Honoré d'Urfé

Twayne's World Authors Series

French Literature

David O'Connell, Editor
University of Illinois

TWAS 698

Honoré d'Urfé

By Louise K. Horowitz

Rutgers University, Camden

Twayne Publishers • *Boston*

Honoré d'Urfé

Louise K. Horowitz

Copyright © 1984 by G.K. Hall & Company
All Rights Reserved
Published by Twayne Publishers
A Division of G. K. Hall & Company
70 Lincoln Street
Boston, Massachusetts 02111

Printed on permanent/durable acid-free paper and bound in the United
States of America.

Library of Congress Cataloging in Publication Data

Horowitz, Louise K.
  Honoré d'Urfé.

  (Twayne's world authors series ; 698)
  Bibliography: p.
  Includes index.
  1. Urfé, Honoré d', 1567–1625—Criticism and
interpretation.   I. Title.   II. Series: Twayne's world
authors series ; TWAS 698.
PQ1707.U7H6   1984   843'.4   83-26454
  ISBN 0-8057-6545-X

For Bob and Esther

Contents

About the Author

Louise K. Horowitz is associate professor of French at Rutgers University, Camden, and a member of the Rutgers, New Brunswick Graduate Faculty. She taught previously at the University of Rochester and the City University of New York, from which she received a doctoral degree in 1973. A former Woodrow Wilson Fellow, a member of Phi Beta Kappa, and a recipient of a fellowship from the American Council of Learned Societies, Professor Horowitz is the author of Love and Language: A Study of the Classical French Moralist Writers, published in 1977 by Ohio State University Press. She has also contributed articles and reviews to diverse scholarly journals, including the French Review, French Forum, the Romanic Review, and Dada/Surrealism. From 1977 to 1980 Professor Horowitz served as book review editor in literary history and criticism for the French Review.

Preface

A study of Honoré d'Urfé's work is, alas, no neat and
tidy matter. Massive in length and scope, L'Astrée,
d'Urfé's principal opus, defies critical surehandedness.
The reading experience alone is baffling. How can one
keep track of so many characters? Or remember the beginning of a tale first narrated two or even three volumes
earlier. Given the many different representative narrators, sometimes for one story alone, how does one recall
who is speaking? L'Astrée is both fragmented and
continuous. The main characters' stories cross d'Urfé's
four volumes: sometimes hundreds of pages separate one
section of a tale from another. What divides these tales
are yet more stories, some brief, others long, some
limited to one volume, others weaved discontinuously
throughout the immense text.

In short, there is no center. The work's title as it
has come down to us is falsely unifying, for the story of
Astrée (and Céladon) is only one more tale, hardly any
more "significant" than that of Diane and Silvandre, of
Hylas, of Galathée, of Phillis and Lycidas. Among the
"minor" tales, there is no objective way to single out
one over another. The decision to focus on certain among
them is therefore strikingly arbitrary. Indeed, it is
far easier to imagine a whole series of books on d'Urfé
and L'Astrée than to conjure up a single, comprehensive volume. Recent critical efforts testify to this
sense of being overwhelmed by the text. Disparate in
vision, these essays are as fragmented as the novel
itself. Yet, each makes a partial contribution to
"grasping" a frustrating work, and perhaps these nonglo-
bal studies reflect the only way to experience d'Urfé's
writing. In any case, the present volume modestly offers
a discussion of some of the important issues concerning
d'Urfé and his works, especially L'Astrée, while
anticipating that the years to come will see a burgeoning
of critical analyses, no doubt varied in topic and
approach.

Following a preliminary examination of the personal,

intellectual, and social forces involved in the composition of d'Urfé's works, I will pursue a detailed analysis of L'Astrée, focusing on the major stories with reference to several secondary tales as well. How d'Urfé systematically conveys, and then subverts, the metaphysical speculation devoted to questions on love inherited from the Middle Ages and the Renaissance, will occupy a major section of this study. As for the themes of L'Astrée, one in particular—disguise—strikes me as so important that I have devoted an entire chapter to it. Through this traditional literary device, d'Urfé not only constructs his plot, but most importantly, creates the erotic anticipation that is the essence of romance.

The remainder of the study will concentrate on structural and narrative problems: the role of the intercalated tale; how d'Urfé creates a polyphonic, yet paradoxically, undifferentiated narrative voice; and how he utilizes written and oral forms, other than traditional narration, to vary (while simultaneously reinforcing) the diegesis.

Such an appraisal is in no sense exhaustive. Nonetheless, it has the advantage of including a fair number of issues inevitably raised for an understanding of L'Astrée and its author, issues which should continue to provoke further critical examination.

All translations from the French are my own. For rapid and skillful translation of secondary material in Italian, valuable for my understanding of L'Astrée, I am indebted to my father, who undertook to help with real verve and sincere interest.

The Rutgers University Research Council generously furnished the financial support permitting me to complete this study.

Louise K. Horowitz

Rutgers University, Camden

Chronology

1567   11 February, Honoré d'Urfé, son of Jacques d'Urfé and Renée de Savoie, baptized in Marseille. Spends early years at château de la Bastie in Forez region of southeastern France.

ca. 1577–1584   Student at Jesuit Collège de Tournon. 1583, composes La Triomphante Entrée de très illustre Dame Magdeleine de la Rochefoucauld.

1589   Joins the Catholic League.

1594   1 October, death of brother, Antoine.

1595   16 February, arrested in Feurs by political enemies. Leaves for Savoy. 15 August, present at death of close friend, the duke of Nemours, in Savoy. September, second arrest at Montbrison. In prison works on the first book of the Epistres Morales, recounting his personal and political misfortunes.

1596   Released from prison. Leaves France for Savoy where he completes his pastoral poem, Le Sireine.

1598   Epistres Morales, first book.

1599   May, marriage between Honoré's brother, Anne d'Urfé, and Diane de Châteaumorand is annulled. Acquires Virieu-le-Grand and Châteauneuf. Virieu, in the Annecy region of Savoy, remains a preferred residence. June, released from the Ordre de Malte. August, completes epic poem, La Savoysiade, first book.

1600   15 February, weds former sister-in-law, Diane de Châteaumorand.

1602   Visits Paris with wife. Reconciliation with Henri IV.

1603   Epistres Morales, first and second books published together.

1605-1607   Lives with Diane de Châteaumorand alternately in Paris, at Virieu-le-Grand, and at Châteaumorand.

1606   Completes La Savoysiade, final book. With François de Sales forms the "Académie Florimontane," a literary society in the Annecy region.

1607   L'Astrée, first part.

1608   Epistres Morales, complete in three books.

1610   L'Astrée, second part. Diplomatic mission at Turin (Court of Savoy) on behalf of the French.

1614   Separates from Diane de Châteaumorand. Lives at Virieu-le-Grand.

1619   L'Astrée, third part.

1625   April, participates in War of the Valteline. Receives the "Privilège du roi" for his pastoral play, La Sylvanire. 1 June, dies at Villefranche. Remains are transported to Forez.

1626   8 March, death of Diane de Châteaumorand.

1627   Publication of fourth part of L'Astrée by Baro, d'Urfé's secretary. Posthumous publication of La Sylvanire.

Chapter One
Honoré d'Urfé: His World

Enveloping Honoré d'Urfé is a legend that not only adds romance and mystery to his life, but also, for generations of critics, has helped to explain the genesis of his work. L'Astrée, as scholars from the seventeenth century on have allowed, is the fictionalized embodiment of the long, frustrating, and passionate attachment Honoré d'Urfé experienced for the wife of his older brother, Anne. Accordingly, Diane de Châteaumorand is transformed, and split, into the two principal female figures of the novel: Astrée and Diane. And the two major male protagonists, Céladon and Silvandre, are seen as the incarnation of Honoré himself, long the frustrated lover.

"Keys" to L'Astrée circulated throughout the seventeenth century, while the eighteenth century only repeated the conventional wisdom: the subject of L'Astrée was Honoré d'Urfé's own troubled tale. Diane de Châteaumorand, wed in 1574 to Anne d'Urfé, who was to remain impotent throughout their marriage, loved the younger brother, Honoré, and he reciprocated her affection. Their not-so-secret romance caused considerable alarm in the d'Urfé family; Honoré was sent away. But when, twenty-five years later, the union between Anne and Diane was annulled, Honoré d'Urfé finally was able to marry her.

The years of frustration d'Urfé was forced to endure because of his love for Diane, no doubt contributed to the writing of L'Astrée, the Epistres Morales, and his pastoral poem, Le Sireine. But especially L'Astrée is so complex that one biographical fact, however enticing, cannot sufficiently explain the totality of the work. L'Astrée, self-referential and hermetic, is above all a literary event. At times, moreover, it seems the product of a civilization, of an epoch, rather than of one man. And its encyclopedic nature may thus best be conveyed by describing the world of the man who wrote it.

1

Forez

"All the old world poured into all the new" (1).   That
is how Gérard Genette has described L'Astrée.   By
date, technically, a work belonging to the seventeenth
century, to the dawn of classicism, d'Urfé's novel is
truly a product of the Renaissance—as is d'Urfé himself.   The area in which he matured—Forez, in southeastern France, near Lyon—was an important cultural center.
Lyon, after all, was second only to Paris as a town where
artistic and literary production flourished.   The château of the d'Urfé family, La Bastie, enlarged and
decorated in the Italian style by Claude d'Urfé,
Honoré's grandfather, was both in form and function a
symbol of Renaissance French culture.   Under Claude, La
Bastie became an important center to the area's artists
and writers.   Claude d'Urfé himself was the stereotypical Renaissance patron: both wealthy and highly cul-
tured, he was a devoted student and supporter of art and
literature, and was closely associated with the writers
who frequented the court of both François I and Henri
II.   The family domain had an extensive library, one of
the largest in sixteenth-century France, acquired primarily through Claude's marriage to Jeanne de Balsac, and
which no doubt was an important educational source for
Honoré d'Urfé and his brothers and sisters.   In the
Oeuvres morales et spirituelles, Anne d'Urfé has
described his own educationally rich experience at La
Bastie, and Honoré d'Urfé's most recent intellectual
biographer, Maxime Gaume, believes that the younger
brother, too, obviously benefited from the extraordinari-
ly cultivated world of the château (2).
    Beyond La Bastie, the whole Forez region offered
fertile ground for an inquisitive, developing mind.
Despite the religious wars between Catholics and Huguenots which tore France apart, the second half of the
sixteenth century in Forez was intellectually vital.
Montbrison, the capital city, was widely known for its
literary production, especially for its poetry.   Around
the writer Loys Papon flourished a school of poetry heavily influenced, as might be expected, by Italian literature.   Anne d'Urfé became one of the group's most
outstanding poets, and Honoré himself, while less tal-
ented for verse than his older brother, also composed
prolifically.

History also was a strong attraction for some of the Montbrison group, especially for Loys Papon's brother, Jean, and it is likely that Honoré d'Urfé, when composing L'Astrée, relied heavily on their knowledge to describe the past days of his province. Fondness for Forez marks d'Urfé's work, as history combines with legend, and both with personal reminiscence, to produce an image of the province as a French Eden (3).

Formal Study

As outstanding as was the milieu that nurtured Honoré d'Urfé in his youth, these surroundings alone did not produce the vast erudition that appears in L'Astrée. In many respects, the novel is a compendium of Renaissance thinking, and this encyclopedic knowledge d'Urfé acquired formally as well as informally. The author of L'Astrée was a student at the Collège de Tournon in the late 1570s through the mid-1580s, and although he left no documentation concerning this period of his life, enough is known about the Collège and Jesuit education in general to sketch a portrait of what d'Urfé must have studied while at Tournon.

Founded in 1536 by Cardinal François de Tournon, a friend of François I, the Collège came under the control of the Jesuits in 1561 and quickly became the most famous of such establishments in the south of France. Like Corneille, Molière, and Bossuet, after him, Honoré d'Urfé benefited from the remarkably successful educational experience offered by the Jesuits. Their ability to reconcile humanism with the principles of the Gospel was unrivaled in the sixteenth and seventeenth centuries. The Collège at Tournon was oriented toward the study of the arts, letters, and philosophy; the last formed the true centerpiece of the Jesuit program, although the teaching of philosophy reflected a rather precise orthodoxy that was not necessarily in vogue among lay intellectuals at the end of the sixteenth century. Aristotle and Saint Thomas formed the obligatory filter through which all of metaphysical thinking passed. Platonic thought was valued only insofar as it helped clarify Aristotle. Nonetheless, reading through the Epistres Morales, it becomes clear that d'Urfé, having mastered Aristotle, was still srongly drawn to Platonic thought, his first exposure to which occurred at Tournon.

Obviously, a Jesuit institution such as Tournon was
deeply interested in the teaching of morals, and primarily in encouraging the students to understand and control
human passions. To supplement the Christian texts, the
Collège proposed readings from Plutarch, Seneca, and
Epictetus. These ancient writers strongly affirmed the
primacy of reason in regulating man's conduct; the Stoicism they preached was particularly compatible with the
teachings of Christianity. The Epistres Morales, as
well as L'Astrée, reflect d'Urfé's early experience
with the ancient thinkers, whom he appears to have read
in depth while at the Collège (4).

Finally, the education d'Urfé received at Tournon
exposed the young man to ancient history, as well as to
the origins of Gaul and of France. Although history
itself was not a formal part of the curriculum, it was
absorbed in relation to the teaching of the Latin texts.
Geography, too, was intimately joined with these other
bodies of knowledge. Thus, to the historical outlook he
had acquired from his close association with the intellectuals of Forez, d'Urfé now added considerable scope and
depth. His teachers and his readings of Pomponius Mela,
Valerius Maximus, Livy, and Caesar widely broadened his
historical knowledge. This formal study was supplemented
by d'Urfé's own readings—begun at Tournon and continued
thereafter—particularly of French Renaissance historians. His favorites appear to have been Claude Fouquet,
Etienne Pasquier, and Girard de Haillan. Not surprisingly, d'Urfé's views correspond to those expressed by many
historians of the time, eager to establish a prestigious
past for Gaul first, then for France. Their efforts were
directed toward diminishing the role of Roman civilization, and allowing the superiority of Gallic culture to
emerge. For Honoré d'Urfé the task was yet more
precise: his wish was to present life in fifth-century
Forez as the apogee of "pure" Gallic civilization.
"Ultimately," writes Maxime Gaume, "the history of Gaul
in L'Astrée, is recounted only insofar as it is able
to corroborate the high quality of the ancestors" (5).
There remains, nonetheless, the thorny question of the
Roman conquest, which, in theory, could destroy the epic
grandeur established by d'Urfé in his novel. Adamas,
the druidic sage of L'Astrée, has a ready answer: the
conquest of Gaul was the result not of Roman military
superiority, but of the quarrels that temporarily divided
and weakened the peoples of Gaul. Adamas's theory is

probably inspired by the writings of Etienne Pasquier, who believed that the divisions and diverse special interests among the Gauls led to the Roman conquest.

Thus, d'Urfé, combining the ancient history acquired at Tournon with the information gleaned at La Bastie and with his extensive readings of Renaissance historians, created a compendium that reflects the state of historical knowledge during the sixteenth century. While ultimately, the power of L'Astrée may not reside in this aspect of the book, d'Urfé did successfully create a true historical framework to accompany the firm metaphysical base.

For d'Urfé, the years at Tournon provided much of the intellectual preparation for his later works. However, while in residence at the Collège, Honoré also wrote his first book. Charged by Tournon's administration to describe the festivities, in April 1583, surrounding the arrival in Tournon of the young wife of count Just-Louis de Tournon, nephew of the school's founding Cardinal, d'Urfé composed La Triomphante Entrée de très illustre Dame Magdeleine de la Rochefoucauld. Published in Lyon the same year, the short work offers an account of several days of celebration accorded the recently married young woman, and its laudatory tone conveys the schoolboy writer's enthusiasm for the happy events (6).

After Tournon: Diane de Châteaumorand and the Catholic League

After completing his training at Tournon, d'Urfé returned to the family residence in Forez, and renewed his friendship with the literary and intellectual figures of the province. The beginnings of L'Astrée may probably be traced to this period of the late 1580s. It was also at this time that he became fascinated with Diane de Châteaumorand, his brother's wife. That this passion served to inspire d'Urfé is unquestionable; whether the author of L'Astrée reproduced his own amorous experience in his novel is less certain. Even the most recent of d'Urfé's biographers have insisted on tightly linking his life to his art, readily interchanging the names of Astrée and Diane de Châteaumorand. But the production of a great work of art transcends biographical material, and the most that may be said in this instance is that

artistic taste coincided with personal events to create a
work devoted to the minute analysis of love in all its
forms.

D'Urfé's life in Forez, however, was far from limited
to his involvement with Diane de Châteaumorand. Not long
after his departure from Tournon, he was obliged to take
up the defense of the Catholic party in its battle
against the Huguenots. In 1576 the Catholics of Picardy
had formed a League to defend themselves against their
Protestant enemies, when Henri III refused to mount a
serious counterattack. The League remained relatively
quiescent until 1584, when, with the death of the king's
brother, the right of succession passed to the Protestant, Henri of Navarre; thereafter, a reformed League
under the Guise family assumed a far more aggressive
stance, as concern for France's future strongly manifest-
ed itself.

The Catholics were determined to prevent Henri of
Navarre from ascending to the throne. Following the
assassination in 1588 of the duke of Guise and the
cardinal of Lorraine, Henri III arrested the duke of
Nemours and the Archbishop of Lyons, ardent defenders of
the Catholic cause in southeastern France. The fury
against the king's policies only increased, and Lyons
joined the League in 1589, becoming the center of opposition for the whole region.

The role of the d'Urfé family in opposing both Henri
III and Henri IV was considerable. Anne d'Urfé joined
the League as early as 1585. Honoré's role (he joined
in 1589) was equally, if not more, significant. For even
when Anne made his submission to Henri IV after the
king's conversion to Catholicism in 1593, Honoré remained loyal to the duke of Nemours, who was unconvinced
by the king's action. After the duke of Nemours died in
August 1595, d'Urfé, now "gouverneur" of Forez, persistently attempted to further the Catholic struggle against
Henri IV (7).

Prison and the *Epistres Morales*

In so many ways, 1595 was a difficult, painful year
for Honoré d'Urfé. He lost his close friend, the duke
of Nemours, shortly after the death of his brother,
Antoine, in October 1594. Moreover, twice during 1595
d'Urfé was imprisoned—once in February, and again in

September. The prison experience and his bereavement
inspired him to compose the Epistres Morales, a philosophically oriented meditation in the form of letters to
an imaginary friend, Agathon. The work is divided into
three books: the first appeared in 1598, the second and
third were written later, and published in 1603 and 1608,
respectively. But it is the first part that bears most
heavily on d'Urfé's difficulties as the century came to
a close. Paradoxically, the precise reasons for the
imprisonments remain hidden in the Epistres Morales.
We learn only that the first was the result of action by
his political enemies, while the second was motivated by
an acquaintance's betrayal. What emerges clearly from
the letters, however, is the writer's deep pain over the
deaths of his brother and friend, and over the prison
terms, as well as his ardent craving for friendship and
moral support.

The Epistres Morales, however, offer more than an
expression of loss and betrayal. They are above all a
hopeful projection of renewed inner strength. The first
book especially is marked by the language of neo-Stoicism, a metaphysical tradition whose base may loosely be
described as a combination of the ancient Stoicism with
Christianity: belief in future happiness, assured by
God, tempers the more rigid Stoic foundation. The moral
that d'Urfé ascribes to Agathon is thus an expression of
happiness, despite the troubles that befall mankind. The
Epistres Morales make clear that reason must be the guiding force in each individual's life, for it alone will
bring man back toward the goodness whose essence is God.

The philosophical foundation for the letters is quite
varied. Stoicism, Epicurianism, Neoplatonism, the precepts of Plutarch, and those of Christianity, all combine
to form a work whose basic affirmation is victory over
the passions, along with a belief in future happiness.
Scholars agree that the second and third books reflect a
more "studied," somewhat derivative analysis of existence, culled from d'Urfé's vast reading. But the first
book stands out as a testimony to the human cycle of
despair and hope (8).

Le Sireine and La Savoysiade

When precisely d'Urfé undertook to write L'Astrée
is not clear. Gaume believes it was in the late 1580s.

Well before 1593, in any case, d'Urfé had formulated the major plot developments of his novel, which at that time he planned to call Les Bergeries. The names of several characters were also determined in this period. But it would be some years until the first part of L'Astrée would appear. Meanwhile, he had completed a pastoral poem, Le Sireine, whose theme and setting bear a distinct resemblance to those of L'Astrée: the joys and anguishes of love in rustic isolation. The poem was completed in November 1596 (although publication was delayed several years), while d'Urfé was residing in the duchy of Savoy. After Honoré's release from prison in early 1596, he had been forced to retire to the duke of Savoy's territory, rather than return to Forez, for he was on poor terms with both Henri IV and his brother Anne, who had earlier made his submission to the French king. Honoré d'Urfé remained in Savoy until his marriage to Diane de Châteaumorand, acquiring the small property of Senoy, and visiting Turin and Milan frequently. In exile virtually from his native country, d'Urfé was able to complete Le Sireine, a work inspired from the Diana of the Spanish poet, Montemayor, and which recounts the separation of Sireine from the shepherdess Diane, and his subsequent return (9).

The coincidence of the heroine's name cannot be overlooked, nor can the story, which seems to reflect d'Urfé's own trying situation with Diane de Châteaumorand. It was perhaps for these reasons that he was drawn to Montemayor's poem. But personal reasons alone could not have sustained the fascination with the pastoral genre that allowed for the composition of Le Sireine and L'Astrée. Evidently, the psychological climate of the pastoral corresponded not only to d'Urfé's immediate situation, but, beyond that, to his intellectual attraction for dissecting the human predicament.

The period in Savoy was an intensely active one for d'Urfé, at least in terms of his literary work. At Senoy, in August 1599, he completed the first book of La Savoysiade, his epic poem celebrating the House of Savoy, a project he would continue to pursue through 1606. La Savoysiade, however, was left unfinished, and, with the exception of one small section of the second book, the nine completed books were never published, although five manuscripts have been preserved in Turin and Paris, the definitive one at the Bibliothèque de l'Arsenal.

The epic mode was prevalent in late sixteenth- and early seventeenth-century Europe. France followed the lead of Italy in attempting to establish a glorious past for the royal houses: between 1600 and 1623, twenty-nine French epic poems were composed. D'Urfé, moved no doubt in part by political considerations, sought his security and fame by creating a work glorifying Bérold, the Saxon prince, chosen by God to be the founder of the magnificent "Maison de Savoie." His sources were primarily books and manuscripts belonging to the House of Savoy (10).

By celebrating the crowning success of Bérold and his son, d'Urfé was glorifying the present ruler, his protector the duke. Perhaps the task was left unfinished and unpublished because Honoré d'Urfé himself came to see that his talent did not lie with the epic format. Despite certain passages conveying heroic grandeur and spirit, La Savoysiade is mired in detail and reflects an effort at imitating ancient Greek and Italian models.

Marriage, *L'Astrée,* and Diplomacy

In 1599, the same year he completed the first part of La Savoysiade, d'Urfé was at last able to visit his home in Forez, in large part because Charles Emmanuel, duke of Savoy, had been reconciled to the French king. It was also at this time that d'Urfé inherited the domain of Châteauneuf, as well as the château of Virieu-le-Grand, which became his preferred residence. Here, he was able to renew his close friendship with François de Sales, with Camus, bishop of Belley, and with the humanist and theologian, Antoine Favre. In 1606, François de Sales and Favre formed the "Académie Florimontane," a literary society composed of theologians, lawyers, and humanists residing in the Annecy region. Courses were offered in arithmetic, philosophy, politics, languages, and music. D'Urfé was an active member of the Academy, finding there both stimulation and companionship.

The year 1599 was an extremely important one in Honoré d'Urfé's personal life. In May, the annulment of his brother's marriage to Diane de Châuteaumorand was finalized. One month later, Honoré obtained his release from the Ordre de Malte, an important religious and military order of knights devoted to combatting infidels.

Without this release, Honoré d'Urfé could not have
married Diane, for the knights were required to take a
vow of chastity. Since 1592 d'Urfé had maintained that
his family had forced him to join the order when he was
only thirteen, three years before the legal age of six-
teen (no doubt because the d'Urfé family had large
debts, as well as several children). The marriage
between Honoré and Diane de Châteaumorand was at last
celebrated on 15 February 1600.

Honoré d'Urfé accompanied his wife to Paris in
1602, and there was reconciled, at least superficially,
with Henri IV. The couple spent the following years
residing alternately in Paris (where d'Urfé divided his
time between the court and the literary circles of the
capital), at Châteaumorand, and in Savoy. D'Urfé
completed the first part of L'Astrée, which was published in 1607. The second part appeared in 1610, the
same year he was sent on a delicate diplomatic mission to
the Court of Savoy in Turin, by Marie de Médicis, who
had become regent following the assassination of Henri IV
(11).

Nonetheless, if his political and literary life was
thriving, his marriage to Diane de Châteaumorand was
not. The fabulous tale thus ends on a sour note, amid
marital quarrels. While there was no formal separation,
after 1614, the couple lived mostly apart; and it was in
the solitude of Virieu-le-Grand that Honoré d'Urfé composed the third part of L'Astrée (published in 1619),
and the fourth (the entirety of which was published in
1627 by his secretary, Balthazar Baro) (12).

In 1625, by now genuinely reconciled with the French
court, as a result of his good diplomatic efforts between France and Savoy, d'Urfé participated in the
War of the Valteline, at the behest of the French king
and the duke of Savoy. The longstanding dispute over
the Valteline, or Val Telline, saw France determined
to control this important valley, which runs north and
then east from Lake Como. In the period 1624-25 France,
under Richelieu, successfully routed the pope's forces,
who controlled the valley, while Spanish troops also
were present in the region. The intervention allowed
France a show of force without the risk of war. D'Urfé
was an active participant in the confrontation, and only
his untimely death in June 1625—most likely from
pneumonia—interrupted his activity (13).

La Sylvanire

L'Astrée was left unfinished. D'Urfé was able,
however, to complete his pastoral play, La Sylvanire,
for which "le privilège du roi" (exclusive publication
rights following examination by official censors) was
accorded on 12 April 1625, less than two months before
his death. The work was published posthumously, in 1627,
but was never presented.

Written in free verse, La Sylvanire owes much to
L'Astrée. D'Urfé even used some of the principal
characters' names from his novel in his play, although
these figures appear in a different context. But the
true model for La Sylvanire, in theme and structure, is
the sixteenth-century Italian theater, particularly
Tasso's Aminta and Guarini's Il Pastor fido, both
translated into French. D'Urfé's play is highly conventional, unlike L'Astrée, which continually transcends
its models. The basic themes of the genre are all present: a shepherdess devoted to hunting; a shepherd who
nonetheless persistently woos her; parental problems; a
false death; and an eventual happy outcome for the two
lovers. A few years later, in 1629, the playwright
Mairet would present his pastoral tragicomedy by the same
name, greatly enriching the characterizations and tighten-
ing up the plot. But even if it is Mairet's play which
has entered the annals of literary history, Honoré
d'Urfé made a significant contribution in his choice of
free verse, an uncommon practice at the time in France,
if not in Italy. What drama and beauty do emerge from
d'Urfé's play are the result of his successful control
of unrhymed verse (14).

Ultimately, however, aside from the Epistres Morales,
d'Urfé's literary contribution beyond L'Astrée is not
a lasting one. But "beyond L'Astrée" is a phrase without meaning, other than strictly historical. L'Astrée
is a universe: to have produced more, of quality, would
have been superhuman. The work is so vast, so detailed,
so complex, and yet, so ordered, that by necessity it had
to be the project of a lifetime.

Chapter Two
L'Astrée: Its World

L'Astrée persistently rejects facile categorizing. It
is a total work, an encyclopedic compendium whose form
reflects its multifaceted exploration of human passion.
Most commonly labeled a novel, L'Astrée often seems
closer to a romance, as defined by Northrop Frye: "The
essential difference between novel and romance lies in
the concept of characterization. The romancer does not
attempt to create 'real people' so much as stylized figures which expand into psychological archetypes" (1).
The characters in L'Astrée vacillate between these two
poles. Diane, for example, is both "real" and archetypal. Her tale is unique, with references to personally
differentiated situations that distinguish her from the
archetypal "cold" shepherdess. At the same time, her
name and her refusal to become involved with Silvandre
place her in a strongly conventional tradition. Similar-
ly, d'Urfé draws a mythologically familiar world of
nymphs in L'Astrée, but these conventional figures are
denied their traditional status. Galathée and her
nymphs not only coexist in the world of mortals; they
also share all human joys, sorrows, and misfortunes.
Their fantasylike qualities fade as they lose their collective, mythical identity and assume distinct, human
characterization.

Literary Sources of *L'Astrée*

For such a world, where identity fluctuates, where the
"real" and the conventional are virtually inseparable,
tracing precise influences and sources for characters and
situations is difficult. D'Urfé's genius is to have
absorbed an immense quantity of reading and to have utilized it in his own writing, but never through facile
imitation. He constantly altered and restructured such
material to form a unique composition. Maxime Gaume has
made a heroic effort at establishing the exact sources
for the principal, and even many secondary, stories of

L'Astrée. But he admits also that as the novel pro-
gresses and shifts, particularly from the third part on,
it becomes increasingly difficult to separate the various
tales and parts of tales, and hence, to trace exclusive
sources for each. Ultimately, however, this may not be a
necessary task. What should emerge from a discussion of
the literary influences contributing to the creation of
L'Astrée is a heightened awareness of the many forms
of writing to which Honoré d'Urfé was exposed. At
times, it seems as if virtually the whole corpus of Occidental literature has found its way into L'Astrée!
While it may be difficult to ascribe precise sources for
each story, it is possible to re-create the literary
atmosphere of d'Urfé's time, and, in particular, to
emphasize those works which contributed markedly to the
composition of L'Astrée.

ANCIENT, MEDIEVAL, AND RENAISSANCE TEXTS. D'Urfé's
opus has long been qualified as a "pastoral novel."
Unquestionably, it is closer in theme and structure to
that genre than to any other. But L'Astrée reflects
more than the preponderant influence of European pastoral
forms, so prevalent in the later years of the sixteenth
century. It also absorbed the atmosphere and concerns of
the chivalric novels inherited from the Middle Ages; of
the ancient Greek adventure romances; and of the Italian,
Spanish, and French nouvelle. At various moments
during the sixteenth century, all these genres were widely read by the cultivated French public; and in a sense,
L'Astrée is the culmination of shifting, diverse
tastes. D'Urfé incorporates, within the basic mold of
the pastoral novel, a vast number of themes and forms.
There is, in short, something for everyone.

During the wars of religion, which long divided Catholics and Huguenots, and which tore apart the nation in
the second half of the century, the French reading audience was fascinated, not surprisingly, by a literature
whose main focus was heroic adventures. The excitement
generated by such works as the Amadis de Gaule series,
and by Ariosto's Orlando furioso, helped to inspire and
divert a people caught up in the nightmare of war. Also
popular at this time were French translations of the
Greek romances, which offered extraordinary adventures
capable of satisfying a readership whose daily life was
no doubt depressingly monotonous and frustrating.

When the war period passed, however, under Henri IV,
an interest developed in a less bellicose, more subtle

and refined literature. In actuality, this was not a new
taste; rather, the religious wars had interrupted a grow-
ing fascination, early in the sixteenth century, for "la
littérature sentimentale," for works devoted to analyzing love. Since, at that time, there was little in the
way of a national literature to satisfy this taste, the
French had turned to Italy and Spain, where this more
"sentimental" tradition flourished. Translations of
Boccaccio had enormous appeal in the early decades of the
sixteenth century, offering readers a subtle portrait of
the human heart. From Spain came an appreciation of the
sacrifices required by absolute devotion. But the religious wars shattered this developing interest, and not
until peace came did the French regain their fascination
for the subtle analysis of the emotions.
    The works they read during the years of the late
sixteenth century were those that no doubt exerted the
greatest sway on Honoré d'Urfé. L'Astrée clearly reflects the tastes of the early and middle years of the
century. The influence of the nouvelle tradition came
perhaps from d'Urfé's exposure to Marguerite de Navarre's
Heptaméron, a work which followed the Italian tradition of combining different "tones" regarding love questions: the range is from the most spiritually elevated to
the most earthy. The Greek romances, with their emphasis
on adventure, and their use of oracles to convey the
imperatives of fate, also influenced the composition of
L'Astrée. Most importantly, the chivalric tradition
continued to impress writers of d'Urfé's generation.
The Amadis, which had brought back to literary life the
world of chivalry, was one of d'Urfé's preferred works,
as was Ariosto's Orlando furioso (2).
    EUROPEAN PASTORAL FICTION. But it was above all the
Spanish pastoral novel and the Italian pastoral play of
the second half of the sixteenth century that were favorites of the French reading public and that came to
dominate d'Urfé's own literary experience. In fact, the
Spanish novel had already incorporated the traditions
represented by the Amadis; thus, d'Urfé's efforts at
wedding "bergerie" and "chevalerie" were not new.
Montemayor's Diana, a pastoral novel that enjoyed great
favor in France, is the single most important influence
on L'Astrée, not only for its successful mingling of
chivalric and pastoral themes, but also for its setting,
themes, and structure. The power of the Diana was felt
even before the first French translation appeared in

1578. Cultivated Frenchmen who had mastered the Spanish language read the work first in its original form. Success was immediate and prolonged. The Diana was translated several times, not only the seven books written by Montemayor, but also the two sequels of Alonzo Perez and Gil Polo.

One other Spanish work additionally stands out as having exhibited a strong influence on d'Urfé. While Cervantes's novel, Galatea, was never translated into French, large numbers of aristocrats well versed in the Spanish tongue, which was in vogue at that time, were able to read and admire this 1585 work. Like the Diana, Cervantes's novel enjoyed huge popularity, in large part for its famous "discussions" on love issues.

Shortly after the Spanish novels caught on in late sixteenth-century France, Italian pastoral dramas captured the fancy of the public. Tasso's Aminta was the clear favorite. First performed in 1573, a French edition in Italian appeared a decade later, quickly followed by three translations. Also greatly admired was Guarini's play, Il Pastor fido, which French women in particular enjoyed. Both works proposed a far more delicate and subtle analysis of love than the French audience had known for a long time.

The pastoral genre, both novel and play, continued to predominate during the reign of Henri IV. Its theme of the purification of love satisfied a public with the peace of mind to reflect on the passions. Nonetheless, despite a real interest in this literature, the pastoral novel never developed successfully in France. In 1571, the writer Belleforest had produced his Pyrénée, which was followed by the Bergeries de Juliette of Nicolas de Montreux, the Philocalie of Ducroset, and de Favre's Bergerie Uranie, in 1598. Between that date and the publication of the first part of L'Astrée in 1607, no other pastoral novel appeared. The genre seems only to have been successful in France as a dramatic form; even the best known of the novels, Nicolas de Montreux's Bergeries de Juliette, is stilted and derivative, lacking in psychological depth. L'Astrée thus stands out as a unique contribution in French literature. Absorbing the material offered by its Spanish and Italian predecessors, d'Urfé's novel moved beyond them, to form a vastly enriched world for an excited reading public, which reciprocated by creating a veritable cult around Astrée, Céladon, and their friends (3).

Pastoral Conventions

THE SETTING. Earlier Italian pastoral novels had
created a country setting so idyllic that the "real"
world of day-to-day labors scarcely disturbed it. More
realistic in its format, the Spanish novel had allowed
the shepherds and shepherdesses to fulfill daily chores
for their flocks. D'Urfé rejects, to some degree, this
portrayal of workaday life, but the shepherds' world in
L'Astrée is not wholly idyllic either. The flocks
are, occasionally at least, a concern and obligation.
The pastoral genre, however, in its insistence on a metaphysical, rather than civic state, cannot allow true
peasant activities to dominate (4). The retreat to the
country reflects the author's wish to create a universe
obviously free of exterior troubles. In this fashion,
the human heart and its troubles and joys may become the
sole focus.

The preferred domain of the countryside had a clear
historical base when d'Urfé began L'Astrée. War-torn
France saw in the retreat to pastoral peace a psychological release. But if the locus of L'Astrée remains at
heart an Arcadian paradise, it is, nonetheless, a region-
ally precise world, quite unlike the vague setting of
earlier pastoral fiction. The nonpastoral novel of the
time was highly nationalistic in its insistence on a
French setting, and d'Urfé clearly followed this tradition. L'Astrée is geographically accurate, to the
point that towns, villages, and rivers may readily be
located on a map. This is not to say that the pastoral
atmosphere of the novel is vitiated. Quite the contrary:
d'Urfé's originality is to have idealized his native
Forez, endowing it with Edenic qualities, while maintaining a setting more in keeping with the interests of a
sophisticated reading public accustomed to the specifically French atmosphere which prevailed in other fiction of
the time. Forez emerges as an historically determined,
geographically fixed region, and, at the same time, as an
almost mythical paradise. D'Urfé successfully inter-
twines the dream with the reality, thereby establishing a
sense of "otherworldliness" right at home (5).

PLOT AND STRUCTURE. The innovations of L'Astrée
are not at the fundamental level of plot. The two
primary tales—involving Céladon and Astrée, and
Silvandre and Diane—adhere, superficially at least, to

the conventions of pastoral literature. The novel's
originality comes from d'Urfé having endowed his characters with far greater psychological depth and subtlety
than his predecessors had achieved in their writing. He
continually moves beyond the conventions of the genre,
creating a work that is pastoral primarily in its fundamental forms, but which also successfully transcends the
theme and structure of earlier works. Nonetheless,
Spanish pastoral fiction had established a basic plot
along with a fixed organizational structure, and in these
areas d'Urfé followed faithfully.

The essential plot of pastoral writing may loosely be
described as a prolonged love story between a shepherd
and shepherdess, where emotional satisfaction is held in
check until the very end. Nonconsummation is the primary
theme, and it becomes the primary narrative structure as
well: without this frustration, the story, as such, may
not proceed. It is, moreover, this erotic suspense that
surely accounts for much of the genre's appeal. Obstacles to a satisfactory outcome are everywhere: exterior,
often, in the form of parental disapproval; and internal,
in the solitary life chosen by the hero, when the secret
relationship between shepherd and shepherdess is shattered by the efforts of a jealous rival. Erotic content
is veiled, but nonetheless real, for the hero frequently
has the occasion to spy on his beloved while she is in a
state of near undress. Eventually, the tale winds its
way to a happy conclusion, with the expectation of a
marriage.

While the hero is separated from his shepherdess, he
partakes in various adventures designed to show both his
worth and his superior background, for often he is himself a disguised knight who has retreated to the "pure"
world of the countryside, or, at least, a descendant of a
noble family. Episodes that owe much to Arthurian-type
romance intrude frequently into the bucolic world, where,
otherwise, the primary "activity" is to discuss endlessly
the fine points of loving. Enveloping these two preoccupations of talk and prowess is an atmosphere of supernatural phenomena and bizarre artifice, which, in fact,
exists both in Spanish pastoral literature and in Arthur-
ian romance. It would seem that the pastoral genre
absorbed the tendency of romance to employ mythical and
magical symbols, although in the hands of Honoré d'Urfé
this supernatural world is greatly reduced. The "outer"
symbol remains; its mythical power fades. The famous

Fontaine de Vérité d'Amour, responsible for the woes of
L'Astrée, seems oddly conventional, free of the suggestive powers traditionally linked to this water symbol.
Still, d'Urfé retained at least the structure of certain supernatural phenomena, thereby ensuring a positive
reaction from a readership nostalgically fond of a
magical atmosphere.

Along the pastoral way, a host of other characters
appear: shepherds who are either friends of or rivals to
the hero, shepherdesses who want no part of love with
men, aggressive strangers, magicians, priests, and wise
old men, sometimes hermits, who offer hospitality and
help, both physical and moral. The characters are frequently in a state of disguise, thereby engendering
dramatic excitement, and also covert erotic adventure.
Various secondary figures not only offer support, but
sometimes problems, for the hero and heroine. Frequently, we "hear" their own stories as well, and in great
detail, for the intercalated tale is a primary structural
form of the pastoral novel. Varying in degrees of independence, these stories may reflect directly back on the
major one, or be related only thematically to it.
D'Urfé was particularly brilliant at manipulating interwoven stories, and in L'Astrée he offers a host of
variations: some tales are closely linked to the narratives of the principal characters, while others serve
primarily as a constant reminder of the work's obsessive
theme: the difficult world of passion.

On the level of narration, pastoral literature, as
inherited and practiced by Honoré d'Urfé, also offers a
conventional format. The narrative voice is often "dispersed" among various characters; no one probably was
more adept at this polyphonic illusion than the author of
L'Astrée. At the same time, to advance the plot, and
to vary the potentially monotonous prose narration,
writers of pastorals often used letters, poems, and
songs, whose themes, of course, reflected directly back
on those woven in the primary text. In some ways,
L'Astrée, which makes extensive use of letters, seems
almost an epistolary novel, so much does the plot depend
upon the successful, aborted, or interrupted exchange of
missives.

Such are the essential conventions of pastoral literature. The remainder of this chapter will treat the specific conventions of L'Astrée. D'Urfé's debt to his
predecessors is substantial. Not that L'Astrée is a

facile imitation of earlier works: d'Urfé consistently transcended the "givens" of pastoral fiction. But his originality will surface best if his work may be viewed within a specific tradition. D'Urfé subverts, even violates, the pastoral code; but not without first carefully re-creating it (6).

The Setting of *L'Astrée:* Forez

Forez is a "theater." So says Honoré d'Urfé in his introductory pages, directly addressed to Astrée. D'Urfé's praise of his native land—"there is something so countrylike in the very name of Forez, a region which seems to invite everyone to spend the rest of his days there, particularly along the banks of the Lignon river" (7)—is as conventional as the rustic setting and costumes of a pastoral play. The author of L'Astrée makes clear from the start that his novel does not portray true peasant life. His characters are peasants only through their literary link to the pastoral tradition, and this status frees them from class-based social typing. Moreover, as d'Urfé quickly explains, the shepherds and shepherdesses of L'Astrée are not so by birth. Their ancestors, born into a superior social rank, abandoned court life, preferring the country so as "to live a gentle life, free of constraint" [1:7]. Since the self is in a state of fundamental disguise, costume and language may reflect not the reality of the peasant condition, but the symbolic, artistic representation of that world.

The "setting" is fifth-century Forez. The Franks dominate the area, as Roman control has finally begun to falter. All the action of L'Astrée occurs in this common meeting ground for the scores of characters: both native residents and various unhappy figures come from afar to resolve their difficulties in love and life. The Forez of the shepherds and shepherdesses offers to all a place where the affairs of the heart may surface in isolation, and where, in turn, the heart may eventually be healed.

Traversing the region is the river Lignon, so important to L'Astrée that it is almost a "character" in its own right (8). The Lignon is first the narrator's confidant, as he recounts early in the third volume; and thus it shares his pains, torments, and joys. This

passage—"Author to the river Lignon" [3:5-7]—has been
viewed traditionally as basically autobiographical, with
d'Urfé reflecting on his tempestuous relationship with
Diane de Châteaumorand. There may be some truth to this
perspective. But the terms the "author" employs to describe his feelings toward the river, and those chosen to
depict how various characters relate to the Lignon, are
strikingly similar. Pastoral literature requires the
strong presence of a river or stream, and d'Urfé's
description adheres faithfully to this tradition. In
L'Astrée, the Lignon becomes a superb witness to the
principal narrator's life, as well as to that of the
book's characters. Astrée herself, in the third part of
the novel, recognizes that she can hardly bear the sight
of this river, "which had been a witness to both the joys
of the past and to the start of her present misery" [3:
555], just as the author-narrator at the beginning of the
same volume confides that the Lignon has seen the high
and low moments of his great passion. The river is thus
the eternal witness, its special place assured by all the
characters', including the narrator's, relationship to
it.

The Lignon, however, is more than a witness of events
and emotions. Geographically, it divides the two regions
of Forez that are of importance in L'Astrée: the left
bank, where reside the shepherds and shepherdesses, and
the right, where may be found the residence of Adamas,
the palace of Isoure of Galathée, and Marcilly castle,
home of the nymph queen, Amasis. A bridge, "le pont de
la Bouteresse," connects the two banks, although in
spirit they remain distinct. As Maxime Gaume has written, the left bank, inhabited by the shepherds, is
completely free of the political and social constraints
imposed by court life, which so often mar the lives of
the right bank inhabitants (9). Galathée and Amasis
need contend not only with warring passions, but also
with warring political factions and rivals. The main
characters cross and recross the bridge, thereby extending their existence to include, principally, the dangers
of the heart, as well, secondarily, as those imposed from
the outside.

A description of loci would be incomplete without the
work's unifying symbol: "la Fontaine de Vérité
d'Amour" ("the Fountain of Love's Truth"). This banal
water symbol is no longer invested with the awesome mythical power traditionally associated with a fountain. The

water itself is not suggestive, and is free of any association with the female spirit—maternal or sexual. This
is not water which elementally inspires, calms, or terri-
fies. Rather, the fountain of L'Astrée is a useful
image serving to convey concretely the novel's metaphysical base. Whoever peers into the alluring water "sees
his mistress, and if he is loved by her, he sees himself
standing near, but if she loves another, it is that person's reflection which will appear" [1:93]. The explanation for this astounding property is that the fountain
interprets the soul of those who love; and a true lover's
soul is transformed into the person he desires. The
water surrenders the image of each loving soul; one sees
not himself but the beloved with whom he shares a perfect
union. The Platonic belief in the transformation of the
soul, of the unity inherent to true love, is one of the
fundamental principles of d'Urfé's novel, and the fountain is the concrete symbol of this metaphysical construct.

Unfortunately, the fountain's unusual powers have
temporarily been suspended. Prior to the beginning of
L'Astrée, Clidaman had flown into a rage upon discovering, via the fountain, that the nymph Silvie did not
reciprocate his affection; he conspired with a druid to
break the fountain's spell. Now, as L'Astrée opens,
the fountain is guarded by two unicorns and two lions
whose task it is to attack anyone who seeks the fountain's help. Of course, it is not truly unfortunate that
the fountain is temporarily inoperable as a source of
revelation. Were it not, there could be no novel, for
L'Astrée is cast in doubt—doubt so great that it
risks destroying the moral foundation of the novel—and
it is precisely doubt that the fountain was able to oblit-
erate. Only when the fountain exerts its magical charm
once more—an event that will occur with the sacrificial
death of the two most perfect lovers—may the diverse
characters discover their true fate.

Retreat from the Court

To the rustic retreat of Forez came the ancestors of
Céladon, Astrée, and their family and friends. Weary
of life at the court, eager for a more tranquil existence, they chose to abandon their status as "chevaliers"
and to assume the identity of shepherds. D'Urfé him-

self, given the political and religious problems his
family had experienced, probably had little personal
fervor for court life. Both L'Astrée and the Epistres Morales convey a strong anticourt sentiment. But
criticism of the world of the court was also a tradition
in sixteenth-century Europe. Castiglione had shown with
The Courtier what the ideal gentleman of the court
should be; and writers throughout the century continued
to depict both the ideal and the seamier reality.

Even the idea of creating shepherds and shepherdesses
as descendants of "chevaliers" who had earlier abandoned
the court was not original with Honoré d'Urfé. One
finds this theme in the Spanish pastoral novels, and
d'Urfé's use of the anticourt motif is clearly part of a
literary tradition, one, moreover, that is essential to
the success of his story. Through this conventional
format, noble essence could illuminate peasant status,
thereby negating the potentially disquieting concept of
class which pastoral fiction traditionally held in check.
This is not to say that L'Astrée is a classless novel
—far from it. Awareness of social status is one of the
strong forces in the novel, and class distinction, as
Jacques Ehrmann has shown, is carefully preserved. The
nymph Galathée persists in wooing Céladon because she
refuses to believe that he could prefer Astrée, a mere
"country beauty" [2:289], to herself. And Diane is kept
from considering Silvandre as a marriage prospect by her
mother's objection to his uncertain background. The
social distinctions of the "real" world are thus sancti-
fied by d'Urfé for whom the only utopia is a moral one;
and on that level alone he posits the superiority of the
shepherds' lives (10). Nonetheless, despite his insistence on inner, moral perfection, d'Urfé allows his
major characters a hidden social status: living as shepherds, they are in essence nobility, and thus maintain a
superior class base.

Religion in *L'Astrée*

One further issue is significant for grasping the
world of L'Astrée. Druidism is ostensibly the novel's
religious foundation, and the attention d'Urfé gives to
this question has long intrigued some scholars. For the
modern reader, however, the pages describing druidic
customs may be the least interesting of L'Astrée. Two

issues seem worthy of special note, however: d'Urfé's
insistence on druidic purity, and the curious link druidism, as he describes it, shares with Catholicism.
D'Urfé had a nationalistic goal in mind when he
stressed in L'Astrée that Gaul remained relatively
free of Roman influence in religious matters. For the
author of L'Astrée, druidism was never contaminated by
Roman pagan beliefs, particularly in Forez, which better
than any other area preserved its religious purity.
Honoré d'Urfé's position in this matter, however, is at
odds with the bulk of historical scholarship. Even highly nationalistic sixteenth-century French historians
concede that Gaul did come under the influence of pagan
Roman religious practices. D'Urfé's portrait of an
untainted Forez undoubtedly served a dual purpose: on
the one hand, he continued the praise of his native
region as a superior area, morally as well as geographically; on the other, he meshed the excellent qualities of
the fictional Forez in the matters of the heart with
those of the soul. As a composite construct, Forez is
perfect.

But druidism, as depicted by Honoré d'Urfé, is less
exotic than might appear on the surface. At times, it
bears a real resemblance to Catholicism, particularly as
d'Urfé transforms druidic polytheism into Christian mono-
theism. The Gauls worshiped several gods; d'Urfé
learned their names—Bélénus, Hésus, Tharamis, and
Tautates—from the French historian Claude Fauchet's
Antiquitez. But this knowledge is altered significantly in d'Urfé's work. In the bark of an oak tree at the
temple Céladon builds for Astrée are inscribed the
names of these Celtic gods, but at the point where the
branches converge appears the name Tautates. Adamas carefully explains to Céladon that there is only one god,
Tautates, and that the words Hésus, Tharamis, and
Bélénus are there to demonstrate that one must love God
under these names as well: "These three names signify
three figures, who comprise one God: THE ALL POWERFUL
GOD, THE MAN GOD, AND THE PURIFYING GOD. The All
Powerful God is the Father, the Man God is the Son,
and the Purifying God is the love of both, and all
three form a Tautates, that is, a God" [2:327]. Nothing
could more explicitly convey the Christian mystery of the
Trinity than the above. Catholic dogma frequently appears in d'Urfé's discussion of druidism. Moreover, as
Maxime Gaume has shown, d'Urfé pointedly mentions how

druids were often subject to persecution, thereby offering an uncomfortable parallel with the martyrdom of certain Catholics in sixteenth-century France.

Religion in L'Astrée is thus a complex issue, offering both a heady exoticism and a parallel with contemporary affairs. Most significantly, however, Forez is a religious paradise, for here especially has the purity of druidic traditions been maintained, and here, too, has religion assumed a profane connotation. According to the theories of Renaissance Platonism which so strongly influenced Honoré d'Urfé, divine love and human love share a fundamental assumption of unity, on the one hand with God, on the other with the beloved (11).

Conclusion

The pastoral format, conditioned by existing knowledge of druidism and by a variety of metaphysical traditions, is the essential mold for L'Astrée. But in no way should this mold be determined as the exclusive one for d'Urfé's novel, which reflects literary traditions culled from antiquity, the Middle Ages, and European-wide Renaissance fiction. Such a variety of forms suggests a work that perhaps should remain unlabeled, for no one term—indeed, not even several terms—will ever adequately convey its encyclopedic nature. L'Astrée is a radical work, one which challenges all critical efforts to stabilize, situate, and name. But the critic's frustration is only a product of the novel's tremendous energy, which may best be appreciated by accepting forthrightly the book's unstable nature.

Chapter Three
L'Astrée: The Story

Background information of an essentially historical and literary nature is vital to an understanding of the composition of L'Astrée. Without it, a reader is left with the impression that this vast, unique work surges suddenly out of nowhere. Instead, d'Urfé's work is genuinely the culmination of multifold converging cultural traditions. L'Astrée, however, is a novel, and as such the first question naturally posed by readers is "what is it about?" It is not about druidism, although pages are devoted to the topic. Nor is it truly about a retreat to an idyllic countryside, even though such background information may help to clarify how the characters found themselves in Forez. And it is not about Forez, despite the fact that d'Urfé writes long passages describing and praising his native province. In the long run, L'Astrée is a romance and thereby portrays countless characters, all in love, or falling in love, or falling out of it. This is what L'Astrée "is about."

The Principal Tales

ASTRÉE AND CÉLADON. Astrée and Céladon's long, frustrating tale begins with Céladon attempting a suicidal plunge into the Lignon River. But only a hint is given at this time for the cause of Astrée's anger, which has obliged Céladon to tempt his fate in so troublesome a fashion. D'Urfé alludes briefly in the novel's opening pages to Sémire's betrayal, telling us that it was this ruse which caused Astrée to become enraged with Céladon, but without explaining the nature of Sémire's trickery. Seventeenth-century fiction frequently began in such fashion, jumping into the middle of the story, and creating, as one critic has said, "instant perplexity" (1). Indeed, it is not until much later that the reader learns the precise nature of Sémire's treacherous behavior.

But the beginning in medias res allows for more than

the mere creation of perplexity and curiosity. L'Astrée opens on a note of disintegration, of frustration,
of obscurity, and it is this tone which will mark the
entire work. Characteristic of all romance, this departure from an integrated state to an alienated one is the
very device which allows the work to progress (2). L'Astrée may be seen as a quest for a state of being, once
relatively secure, now (and for the duration of the
novel) lost. Astrée's anger and Céladon's precipitous
jump into the Lignon are only the trigger devices for a
series of obstacles which cumulatively block the union of
the couple.

This is not to suggest that the relationship between
Astrée and Céladon prior to Sémire's betrayal was
completely harmonious. Obstacles to their love were born
with them and are always present. Astrée's father,
Alcé, and Céladon's father, Alcippe, were rivals in
their youth for the hand of Amarillis. The bitterness
engendered by Alcippe's triumph was never transcended.
Thus, strong parental opposition exists to a love match
between the adolescent Astrée and Céladon, with the
result that the young couple has resorted to subterfuge.

In fact, the whole relationship is determined by
feint, even independently of parental problems. Céladon
audaciously initiated the friendship with Astrée by
disguising himself as a woman, in order to act as judge
of the most beautiful shepherdess viewed in the nude. He
awards the prize to Astrée, who, upon learning his true
identity, pretends great anger, although she is clearly
charmed. Once their mutual love is ascertained, the
couple retreats to subterfuge to avoid a parental ban.
They find a secret meeting place, and discover a partial-
ly hollow willow tree which serves them as a place to
exchange letters, while Céladon's hat becomes a portable
mailbox. Eventually, they are forced to pretend that
they love others, so that their parents will harbor no
suspicions. It is this ruse that ultimately engenders
all their problems, for Sémire, jealous of Astrée's
passion for Céladon, is able to persuade the heroine
that her lover is not feigning admiration for a certain
Aminthe, but is genuinely in love with her. Astrée
accuses Céladon of unfaithfulness: he jumps into the
Lignon. And the novel begins its long, winding tale of
obstacle, the prior state of satisfaction (albeit through
subterfuge) having been dispelled.

Tossed about by the impetuous Lignon, Céladon is

thrown onto the river bank, and there is discovered in a
half-drowned state by Galathée and two of her nymph
attendants, Léonide and Silvie. Galathée believes that
Céladon is the young man whom an oracle (who, it will
turn out, is an impostor) has told her she is to wed; she
brings him back to the palace of Isoure to recuperate.
There, Galathée genuinely falls in love with Céladon,
trying everything in her power to dissuade him from
Astrée. Léonide also falls in love with the young shepherd, causing Galathée to accuse her friend of treachery. Eventually, through the help of Adamas (who is also
Léonide's uncle), Céladon escapes from the palace
disguised as a woman, and thereby successfully resists
the seduction attempted by Galathée.

Only the three nymphs and Adamas know that Céladon is
still alive. Astrée and her friends, having found
Céladon's hat, remorsefully conclude that he drowned the
day he jumped into the river. Astrée is deeply de-
pressed, torn by her doubt regarding Céladon's relationship with Aminthe, and by her guilt for having caused his
death. Céladon, alive though he is, refuses to appear
before Astrée now that she has banished him from her
sight. He continues to lead a nomadic, solitary, virtually moribund existence in the woods, where, on the sugges-
tion of Adamas, he builds a temple to the goddess
Astrée, replete with the Twelve Tables of the Laws of
Love. Astrée, meanwhile, convinced she saw Céladon's
ghost one day in the woods (where, indeed, the true
Céladon now lives), constructs a magnificent tomb so
that his wandering soul may find repose.

This state of confused nonfulfillment would surely
continue, were it not for the intervention, yet again, of
Adamas, who devises a unique strategy for the reunion of
the two lovers. Adamas will pass Céladon off as his own
daughter, Alexis, who has been living in a convent for
several years. "She" will live in close proximity to
Astrée, and this ingenious plot will fully realize the
letter of Astrée's ban, if not the spirit: it will be
"Alexis," and not Céladon, whom Astrée will see!
Céladon comes to accept this casuistry, and disguised as
Alexis is able to reside with Astrée, who befriends
"her" instantly. At least on the subconscious level,
Astrée perceives a strong resemblance to Céladon, which
greatly increases her attraction.

The intimacy that the two discover in this ambiguous
set of circumstances is often overlooked, or belittled,

by scholars eager to characterize L'Astrée as "idyllic" or "précieux." But the sections which portray this
strange, polyvalent relationship are among the most
intriguing of the novel—they will be studied in depth
later. For now, it is enough to know that this blissful,
if equivocal, state of affairs, begun in part 2, continues through part 4 (the last part to be composed by
d'Urfé), until both Alexis-Céladon and Astrée are
taken prisoner by Polémas. The latter has undertaken
the siege of Marcilly, where resides the queen nymph,
Amasis. All the novel's principal characters, and many
of the secondary ones, are on hand to protect the queen.
Alexis-Céladon is rescued from Polémas's men, along
with Astrée, and performs valiant deeds in defense of
Marcilly.

The fifth part, traditionally viewed as the conclusion
of the novel, and written by d'Urfé's secretary,
Balthazar Baro, offers at last the reconciliation of the
two lovers, free of the Alexis persona. Initially dis-
mayed upon learning that Alexis is Céladon, for all the
shame she feels about their prior intimacies, Astrée
again banishes her lover, ordering Alexis to die. Then,
remorseful, she seeks death herself: a suicide at the
Fontaine de Vérité d'Amour to prove her true faithfulness and love. But the vicious lions and unicorns protect, rather than sacrifice her, and at the fountain she
is reunited by the god of love with Céladon, who also
has come there to seek his death.

So concludes the major tale of d'Urfé's novel.
Stretched out over five volumes, the story offers none of
the succinctness of this summary. What emerges from reading the entire work is an overwhelming, monotonous sense
of blockage, of increasing frustration, except for certain of the Alexis passages, and even in those instances,
emotional transparency is clouded over by the female
disguise which prohibits sexual union. But satisfaction
is delayed not only by events internal to the dilemma of
Astrée and Céladon. From the reader's perspective it
is halted also by the proliferation of other stories,
which interrupt the continuum of the primary narrative.
The problems of Phillis, Diane, Silvandre, Hylas, and
Galathée also traverse the five volumes, breaking into,
but also reinforcing the Astrée-Céladon narrative.

DIANE/SILVANDRE AND PHILLIS/LYCIDAS. Intertwined with
the tale of Astrée and Céladon are the equally convoluted stories of Diane, Silvandre, Phillis, and Lycidas.

So long and detailed are these narratives that they form
mini-novels within the larger work. Each set of tales is
unique, each is individualized. Yet, through their
themes of doubt, jealousy, fear, and depression, they are
reflections, doubles even, of the Astrée-Céladon
romance. Nor does d'Urfé even attempt to mask this
sense of reflective repetition. Quite the opposite:
Lycidas is Céladon's brother, Phillis is Astrée's
cousin, and the blood links serve to reinforce the
emotional ones. At the point when Astrée and Céladon,
in order to fool their parents, pretend to love other
people, they engage first in an exchange subterfuge with
Lycidas and Phillis, who also are attempting to keep
their romance secret. And just as Astrée comes to distrust Céladon's playacting, so, too, does Lycidas become
jealous of Phillis's pretend relationship with Céladon,
despite the prior agreement.

Indeed, Lycidas reveals himself throughout the novel
to be as impetuously jealous as Astrée. His mind is
grounded in doubt, and like his female counterpart, he
consistently misinterprets signs. Were it not for the
more placid temperament of Phillis, the entire romance
would surely disintegrate, for Lycidas is unable to transcend his jealousy, unwilling to trust.

Phillis is, in fact, radically different from both
Astrée and Diane, her two close friends. A freer
spirit, less tormented, she is willing to bend with the
needs of a love relationship. She is even able to accept
and forgive Lycidas's momentary, but real, infidelity
with Olimpe. Her flexible nature contrasts strikingly
with the absolute standards of both Astrée and Diane,
who banish their lovers on the most whimsical hearsay.
Phillis, in the face of Olimpe's pregnancy, is still able
to accommodate her love for Lycidas. Nonetheless,
Phillis's flexibility in love matters brings her small
reward. Despite her more realistic views, her freedom
from the absolute norms imposed on their lovers by Diane
and Astrée, Phillis's tale, too, becomes one of jealousy
and distrust. Lycidas concludes that Silvandre is in
love with Phillis, and episode after episode relates his
solipsistic anxiety. Like Céladon, Lycidas's refuge
comes to be the woods where he wanders aimlessly in a
depressive fashion, unable to transcend his ingrained
doubt.

At this point, the Phillis-Lycidas narrative meshes so
completely with the story of Diane and Silvandre, that it

is increasingly difficult to separate them. D'Urfé's
stories commonly penetrate one another, with the result
that the characters' worlds become inseparable, duplicating and reflecting themselves seemingly ad infinitum.
Silvandre and Phillis wager as to who may better love
and serve Diane, the most difficult of all mistresses.
She has only loved once, a certain Filandre, who died
rescuing her from the rapacious hands of a vicious Moor.
Having pledged undying love to him at the moment of his
death, Diane will never belong to another. In her rigorous, proud stance, she only repeats the life of her
mother, Bellinde, who also loved once, absolutely. (As
with Alcippe and Céladon, the older generation seemingly
passes on to the younger a gene for difficulties in love
matters, although this link does not make the elders any
more understanding of or sympathetic toward their children!) Diane, however, slowly feels herself attracted to
Silvandre, but she will not give in and allow herself to
love him. He, in turn, having known emotional liberty
all his life, now finds himself passionately in love with
the mistress he had vowed to serve only on a bet.
     As was the case for the strange, equivocal relation-
ship between Astrée and Alexis—where sex roles were so
curiously inverted—the trio of Diane, Silvandre, and
Phillis gives rise to a curious state of affairs. Not
only does Silvandre, who is nicknamed "l'Insensible" for
his prior indifference to women, actually fall in love
with Diane, and vice versa, but Phillis herself serves
Diane so well that it is claimed "no shepherd could
perform any better" [2:293]. She gradually becomes the
"perfect lover," the incarnation of the ideal cherished
by the "courtois" tradition. Diane, meanwhile, persists
in refusing Silvandre, who continues to woo the defiant
shepherdess, although she has by now pronounced an enigmatic judgment as to who better served her. Even when
Diane recognizes and accepts her positive feelings toward
Silvandre, she refuses him on the grounds that his background is unclear, his social rank unknown. In fact, all
Silvandre knows about his background is that in war the
Burgundians brought him to Geneva, and this when he was
only a child. Now he has come to Forez on the advice of
an oracle, where he is to learn the true secret of his
birth.
     Despite Diane's resistance, Alexis-Céladon urges
Silvandre to continue his efforts, although Alexis's
recommendations offer a bizarre note: Silvandre should
pursue Diane, but only as before, when it was all a game.

To diminish the threat to Diane's psychological equi-
librium, Silvandre is merely to pretend that he is in
love with her, as he had done while the wager was
effective. These tantalizing possibilities for pre-
tense and reality becoming one and the same are, however,
negated by the treachery of Laonice (equivalent to that
of Sémire in the Astrée-Céladon narrative), who
tells Diane that Silvandre is really in love with
Madonte. While patently untrue, this rumor causes
Diane the greatest anguish. Her jealousy, which is the
result of her willingness to trust specious hearsay, is
as great as Astrée's, and quite different from Phillis's
reaction upon learning of Lycidas's real infidelity
with Olimpe. The spite and self-destruction that emerge
from this development are fully assumed when Diane
decides to marry Pâris, Adamas's son, even though she
does not love him. The double sacrifice—double, for
Silvandre plans to kill himself—is aborted, however, in
Baro's text, at the Fontaine de Vérité d'Amour. The
god of love appears: he orders Astrée and Céladon's
union, but he also announces that Silvandre is to be
sacrificed by Adamas. At the last minute, Adamas
realizes that Silvandre is really his son, Pâris; the
"other" Pâris, it turns out, is Bellinde's son, and
therefore brother to Diane. "Silvandre" is thus sacrificed, but only symbolically, as he assumes his true
identity as Pâris, and is able to anticipate a match
with Diane.

     HYLAS. The huge success of L'Astrée was due in
large part to the fascinating character of Hylas. The
very portrait of faithlessness, Hylas is a major figure
of the novel, and tales of his amorous adventures are
always cropping up. D'Urfé draws him as the counterpart
to Silvandre, who, more than any other character in
L'Astrée, expresses the Renaissance Platonic concept
of spiritual love. Hylas is overtly interested in the
physical aspect of loving, and he insists that inconstancy is the sincere mark of love. Anything else, he believes is sheer hypocrisy.

     Unlike the other principal figures, Hylas was not
familiar to readers of pastoral fiction. Neither the
Spanish nor Italian writers had so superbly portrayed the
unfaithful lover. Italian pastoral dramatists had overtly portrayed sensual love in the figure of the satyr, but
this seductive creature is quite different from Hylas.
Whereas the satyr frightens girls, Hylas remains seduc-
tively charming, as he draws female after female into his

web. There is, of course, an obvious negative aspect to
this "love 'em and leave 'em" character, for Hylas, charming as he may be, is completely exploitative of women.
Nonetheless, d'Urfé strikingly altered the conventions
of pastoral literature, dispensing with the mythological
satyr and presenting inconstancy in a totally human
format.
"The rule we see that nature has inscribed in all
things . . . teaches us that only diversity makes the
universe beautiful" [4:231]. Placing himself within this
fundamental natural framework, Hylas opts for the greatest variety possible in love matters. Raised as the
spoiled only child of an adoring mother, this native of
Camargues is quickly initiated into seduction. His
stories are all variations on the same theme. Women are
"trapped"—some escape, others experience real heartache.
From Carlis and Stilliane in Provence, he moves on to a
whole series of women in the Lyon region: there are
Aimée, Floriante, Cloris, Circène, Florice, Dorinde,
Cryséide, and even, at one point, Alexis, whom Hylas
fails to recognize as Céladon! It is not until he meets
and falls in love with Stelle that he discovers his true
mate. A young widow, Stelle is as emotionally free as
Hylas, and together they work out a contract of the
twelve conditions of love, which allows them both to love
others and to separate when their mutual ardor has
passed. Their freedom, writes d'Urfé, permits them to
establish a relationship more feeling and more passionate
than any they had known before. Free of constraint,
their attachment grows.
        The role of Hylas in L'Astrée has long been a con-
troversial one. Many scholars have persisted in believing that he represents a challenge to Silvandre's (and
thereby, in their view, d'Urfé's) Platonic orthodoxy.
But nowhere in the novel is this distinction posed,
except perhaps by Baro, but his novel is not d'Urfé's.
The views of Silvandre and Hylas are, of course, contradictory. But d'Urfé simply plays one off against the
other, creating ultimately a moral vacuum, where no
authoritative voice emerges at all.
        GALATHÉE. In many ways, the nymph princess
Galathée's story is a reflection of Hylas's—but with
none of the self-indulgent humor of the latter. By
temperament, she is as impetuous and jealous as Astrée,
unlike the free thinking Hylas, but she does resemble the
iconoclast in her preaching of infidelity, which for her,

as for him, means essential liberty. However, what dis-
tinguishes these two partisans of emotional freedom is
Galathée's need for absolute obedience from her admirers, while Hylas relaxes in Stelle's own liberty. Ultimately, Galathée's constant change of partners reflects
an emotional insecurity more than a philosophical acceptance of individual freedom.

Thus, involved at one time with Polémas, she thinks
nothing of abandoning him for Lindamor, who, in a role
similar to that of Silvandre with Diane, begins to court
her initially only as a game. But fiction quickly becomes truth, and Lindamor and Galathée find themselves
in love, at the expense of Polémas. The two young men
engage in a heated fight; Galathée orders Lindamor to
quit the struggle, but he cannot since at that moment he
risks his own life. Furious that she has been disobeyed,
Galathée abandons her relationship with Lindamor, who
leaves the palace of Isoure, while a false rumor spreads
that he has died. Upon hearing this piece of news, the
self-absorbed Galathée can only wonder if he recalled
her on his deathbed!

In the meantime, Polémas has planned his revenge. He
connives with Climanthe who pretends to be a druid
oracle. The latter then fools Galathée, telling her she
will meet her future husband on a certain day at a speci-
fied location. Polémas is to be there as prearranged,
but he arrives late, and Galathée discovers Céladon
instead, half dead from his plunge into the Lignon. She
takes him with her back to the palace, but Céladon,
always faithful to Astrée, refuses all her advances.
Eventually he escapes, but not without having to hear
Galathée's harangues on both social superiority and the
reality of infidelity.

Polémas, however, refuses to give up hope, not so
much because he truly loves Galathée, but because he
wishes to further his ambitious goals by a prestigious
marriage. In total frustration, he plans to besiege
Marcilly, home of Amasis, Galathée's mother. But
despite his aggressive attack, he is unable to take the
castle; Polémas is in fact killed, and Galathée, in
Baro's work, ultimately becomes a good friend to Céladon
and Astrée, renouncing her former seductive intentions.

Galathée's story is, curiously, seconded by the tale
of her satellite nymph, Léonide. Léonide's position is
primarily reflective. Polémas had once loved her, in
fact, but eventually abandoned her for Galathée, just as

Léonide had earlier left Agis for Polémas! When
Galathée falls for Céladon, Léonide does also, and he
is cause for considerable suspicion and distrust between
the two nymphs. It is, indeed, this constant shifting of
love partners that engenders so much ill feeling, and in
this both Galathée and Léonide share a common pattern.
The stories summarized in the preceding pages form
together the main narrative of L'Astrée. Interwoven,
they are related on the levels of plot, character, theme,
and structure. However, a large number of other tales
interrupt these principal narratives, retarding their
conclusion, but also reinforcing d'Urfé's principal
directions. Given the limits of the present volume, it
would be impossible to summarize them all. Rather, I
have selected a handful of the longest and most significant to recapitulate here. Later chapters will take into
account these tales, along with some others for which
plot descriptions are not strictly necessary.

The Secondary Tales

THAMIRE, CÉLIDÉE, AND CALIDON. Calidon was raised by
Thamire as a son. Both the younger and older man fall in
love with the same girl, Célidée, whom Thamire has
loved since she was a child. Célidée returns Thamire's
affection, and the couple plans to wed. Realizing that
with marriage, Célidée will "belong" to Thamire,
Calidon becomes gravely ill. Unable to bear Calidon's
affliction and sickness, Thamire determines to sacrifice
his own happiness, and promises Célidée to Calidon, who
quickly regains his health. But Célidée wants no part
of a marriage to Calidon; and she also turns against
Thamire who willingly sacrificed her happiness along with
his own.
    A quarrel among the three develops, and ultimately
Léonide becomes the arbiter, concluding that Célidée
should marry Thamire, since they have long loved one
another. Upon hearing this unfavorable judgment, Calidon
again becomes ill, and this time is close to death. At
this point Célidée decides to take forceful action.
She slashes her beautiful face with a diamond, an act
which results in vile permanent scars, and in this desper-
ate gesture assumes the totality óf her situation. For
her there is no loss, since she comes to believe that
physical beauty is a passing grace and one that she will

do without for the sake of inner peace. As expected, Calidon quickly loses interest, now that Célidée is no longer so appealing. Thamire, on the other hand, remains ardently faithful, attracted more to the inner radiance of Célidée than to her former splendid charms.

By the end of L'Astrée, Célidée's face has magically been restored to its former beauty! But throughout L'Astrée, the disfigured face of Célidée is often alluded to as a symbol of unlimited personal freedom.

SILVIE, LIGDAMON, AND LYDIAS. Silvie, the youngest of the three nymphs who figure prominently in L'Astrée, is also the most beautiful. While Galathée and Léonide do everything in their power to woo Céladon, he admits to himself that were he ever to fall in love with someone other than Astrée, it would be with the indifferent Silvie. Perhaps the young nymph's refusal to love or be loved is part of her attraction. Her cruel rigors in refusing Ligdamon, who has adored her since adolescence, her indifference to his subsequent depression and illness, her fear that others will discover his passion, these are the traits of Silvie's personality. Other men, too, are powerfully attracted by her beauty and her obstinate refusal to venture into the domain of love. Aristandre, Guyemants, and Clidaman all succumb, early in the novel, to Silvie's charms.

But Silvie's story is primarily Ligdamon's. Rebuffed by the nymph, Ligdamon leaves for Mérovée's army, is eventually taken prisoner and brought to Rouen where everyone mistakes him for another knight, Lydias, who had killed a rival for the love of a certain Amerine, and who is now to be slain as punishment. Captured, Ligdamon escapes the death penalty only through the good graces of Amerine, who sees him slay two lions and begs that he be allowed to live.

The consequences of this act are nonetheless troublesome for Ligdamon. Amerine truly believes he is her lover, Lydias, and he finds himself obligated to marry her. At the wedding ceremony, however, Ligdamon, ever faithful to Silvie, drinks a poisonous beverage he has prepared, which Amerine also shares. Both fall to the ground.

They are, however, saved from death, and together leave for Forez, where Ligdamon hopes to convince Amerine that he is not Lydias. En route, they are arrested and imprisoned, and Ligdamon is able to escape to Forez only by donning Amerine's clothes.

The real Lydias, meanwhile, had saved himself from the
death sentence by escaping to London. When he returns to
France, however, the governor of Calais, Lypandas, ar-
rests him. The latter arranges a duel for himself and a
relative of Lydias, since he is unwilling to enter into
direct combat with a murderer. A young woman, Mélandre,
who had fallen in love with Lydias while he was in London, dresses up as "le Chevalier Triste," and defeats
Lypandas, thereby freeing Lydias. Mélandre departs without acknowledging her true identity. But Lypandas had
lied; he refuses to free Lydias. Once more, Mélandre
saves his life, assuming Lydias's place in prison and
allowing him to escape. When the latter discovers who
she really is, he undertakes in turn to save Mélandre,
and the two flee together.

Ultimately, however, the tale loses its chivalric
flavor and becomes essentially one of disguise and mis-
taken identity. Ligdamon and Lydias (the names alone are
so alike!) continue to be confused. At Marcilly, the two
are united in battle against Polémas, and eventually
their true identities are revealed. Finally, Mélandre
marries Lypandas, Amerine is accorded to Lydias, and
later, Silvie will accept Ligdamon, whom she has grown to
love only after learning of his supposed death.

DAMON AND MADONTE. This is one of the longest narratives in L'Astrée. Stretched out over the second,
third, and fourth parts, the story of Damon and Madonte
reflects the vast reading experience of Honoré d'Urfé.
Combining tones appropriate to both pastoral and chivalric fiction, this tale is ultimately a novel unto
itself—but one that continues to reflect the basic
themes of L'Astrée. Madonte and Damon are in love,
but Lériane, the young woman who is to watch over
Madonte and report back to those responsible for her,
also falls in love with Damon and becomes violently
jealous of her mistress. Tersandre, a rival to Damon,
passionately loves Madonte, and thus the lovers find themselves menaced by a double threat from outside.

Lériane secretly plots to win Damon for herself. She
pushes Tersandre to declare his love to Madonte, thereby
hoping to incite Damon's jealousy, and she hints to
Madonte that Damon is in love with another woman,
Ormanthe. In effect, Damon becomes violently jealous
upon discovering a letter addressed to Madonte by
Tersandre. The two knights duel, and Damon is wounded.
Lériane, meanwhile, continues her treachery. Ormanthe

has become pregnant and after the child is born in
secret, Lériane claims the child belongs to Madonte.
For this serious breach of conduct, Madonte will die if
her innocence cannot be established by a defender in a
combat situation. An unknown knight, who is Damon in disguise (in a development probably influenced directly by
the Orlando furioso), arrives to assume her defense.
He saves Madonte, but then disappears, without ever
acknowledging his identity.

Damon, we learn from the tale he tells to Galathée,
had not died from the wounds he received in his duel with
Tersandre. Believing Madonte unfaithful (but nonetheless
later prepared to save her life), he had jumped into the
Garonne River, and was rescued from death only at the
last minute. Then, with his servant, Halladin, he trav-
eled all the way to Africa, but without emerging from his
depression. Ultimately, he arrives in Forez where he is
attacked by Polémas, but is saved thanks to the lions at
the Fontaine de Vérité d'Amour. Attacked yet again, he
is rescued by his old rival, Tersandre. Finally, Damon
and Madonte are reunited, as a friendship also begins
between the two men.

CÉLIODANTE, ROSANIRE, AND ROSILÉON. This narrative is
one of the most convoluted of L'Astrée. Less pastoral
in flavor, and also owing less to the chivalric tradition
than many others in L'Astrée, Rosanire and Rosiléon's
story is generally classified as "romanesque" for its
emphasis on an illegitimate birth and subsequent confused
identities. This qualification, however, only highlights
external characteristics; the fundamental themes of
L'Astrée are once more duplicated.

Two sons were born to Queen Argire. The first, whose
father is King Policandre, is illegitimate; the second
son, Céliodante, born from Argire's subsequent marriage
to the king of the Santons, is the legitimate heir.
Greatly attached to her illegitimate child, Argire substitutes one son for the other. The illegitimate son
assumes the name of Céliodante, while the true boy of
that name is abandoned, eventually to be captured by
pirates.

King Policandre, meanwhile, has two daughters,
Rosanire and Céphise, the latter adopted. The king pur-
chases a slave, who happens to be the real Céliodante,
and who falls in love with Princess Rosanire, while
distinguishing himself at the court. He is baptized
Rosiléon, a combination of the name Rosanire, whom he

serves, and the word "lion" because he slew such a beast
one day when it was about to attack the king. Through
his prowess, he quickly rises to become an aid to
Policandre.

At this time, Policandre is warring with the fake
Céliodante, whom Argire has raised as her legitimate
son. This fact, however, is not known by the king, who
is not even aware he fathered a boy by her! This
Céliodante is able to obtain, as part of a peace treaty
between himself and Policandre, the hand of the princess
Rosanire. In reality, these two are half brother and
sister, since Policandre is the father of both, but this
is unknown to all at the king's court. Meanwhile,
Policandre conjures up a match between Rosiléon and his
adopted daughter, Céphise.

When Rosiléon, absent from the court on behalf of the
king, learns of these developments, he returns to demand
the hand of Rosanire. The king refuses, and the story
then assumes a somber tone. Rosiléon refuses to submit
and, in fact, rebels against Policandre's orders, at
least verbally. (Interestingly, the fourth part of
L'Astrée, where Rosiléon's revolt occurs, is marked
by other such rebellions. D'Urfé has firmed up the male
figures in his novel, who no longer submit or become
passively ill; in part 4, they battle for what they
believe is their due.) But because he cannot have
Rosanire, and because he also loses his elevated position, Rosiléon ultimately goes insane. Naturally, by
the end of L'Astrée, the situation is righted. Argire
arrives to confirm the words of a former confidant who is
now at Policandre's court and has at last recognized
Rosiléon as the legitimate son of Queen Argire. In a
reversal of the original plans, Céliodante will marry
Céphise, while Rosiléon, now cured of his madness, will
be granted Rosanire. Policandre marries Argire, both
spouseless now, just as the queen had wished so many
years earlier.

CRYSÉIDE, ARIMANT, AND GONDEBAUD. The story of
Cryséide and her friend, Arimant, is interwoven in the
narrative of Hylas and Cryséide. An important tale, it
nonetheless is limited only to part 3. Cryséide, by
nature suspicious of men and of love, eventually sur-
mounts her doubts to reciprocate the affection of
Arimant. But the women of her region are kept virtual
prisoners, and they must therefore find covert ways to
maintain their amorous relationships. Cryséide and

Arimant's method—one which recalls that of Astrée and
Céladon—is to exchange letters in devotional books. But
Cryséide's mother and family have other plans for her:
they wish her to marry Clorange, an old and deformed
suitor. One relative in particular encourages this
match: Rithimer, a regional governor, who believes he
will readily seduce the young woman if she is unhappily
married. Cryséide attempts to bleed herself to death,
but is saved by her confidante, Clarine. Once recovered,
she is sent by her mother to Rithimer's palace.
Arimant, however, has heard that Cryséide is dead.
He plots to gain access to Rithimer's territory, no easy
task since the governor is an avowed enemy of his own
family. Arimant wishes to kill Clorange, whom he blames
for Cryséide's "death," and then plans to commit suicide. But when he hears that Cryséide is indeed alive
and well, he alters his decision. In the first of many
disguises, Arimant dresses up as a merchant, in order to
reach his friend who is still at Rithimer's palace. He
meets up with Clorange, his rival, and kills him, but is
himself wounded in the struggle. The travesty, meanwhile, continues. Now Cryséide and Clarine dress up as
men and escape with Arimant. All proceeds smoothly, and
we even come to anticipate a marriage, until the powerful
monarch Gondebaud arrives on the scene, attacks, and
leaving Arimant for dead, takes Cryséide prisoner.

Gondebaud (lusting here, as elsewhere in L'Astrée)
quickly falls in love with Cryséide, who loathes him but
fears she cannot risk rejecting such a powerful and capri-
cious male. Arimant, of course, is not dead, and by
disguising himself as his servant, Bellaris, is able to
secure the safety of Cryséide and Clarine. But
Gondebaud still desires Cryséide, whom he finds again,
even after she has escaped and been reunited with
Arimant. A marriage is to occur between Gondebaud and
Cryséide, but at the sacred Tomb of the Two Lovers, the
woman grabs a knife and threatens suicide if he persists
in his plans. As long as she keeps her hand on the Tomb,
according to sacred tradition, no one may touch her.
Arimant arrives, and announcing to Gondebaud that he was
responsible for Cryséide's escape, prepares to die himself. But faithful Bellaris pleads that his master's
life be spared, and Gondebaud, genuinely moved, accords
him both his life and Cryséide.

This narrative is one of the most draining of L'Astrée. Satisfaction, always near, is until the very end

consistently blocked. After all the drama of the
Cryséide-Arimant narrative, Hylas (who himself had
fallen in love with the young woman at Lyon, when she was
prisoner to Gondebaud) can only heap mockery on the rigid
attitudes of the characters, particulary of Cryséide,
who persistently refuses Gondebaud, thereby placing all
in considerable danger.

SILVIANE, ANDRIMARTE, AND CHILDÉRIC. Silviane is the
conventional superior woman, both beautiful and intelli-
gent. She and Andrimarte have loved each other since
they were children. Obstacle, however, is the hallmark
of d'Urfé's novel; and despite the fact that the young
couple is actually wed early in the story under the protection of King Mérovée, this happy union risks being
destroyed by the lustful intervention of Childéric,
Mérovée's son. The prince falls in love with Silviane,
so much so that unbeknown to her, he has her portrait
painted, and ritualistically embraces it each day.

This fetishism does not go unnoticed by Silviane, and
sensing that her person has effectively been violated,
she throws the portrait into the fire. But Childéric
remains obsessed with Silviane, to the great dismay of
Andrimarte. When the latter must leave the court to
serve the king, Silviane is left completely exposed to
Childéric's advances. The king, aware of his son's
troublesome intentions, tries to dissuade him from
further actions, and tells Childéric that he is not to
disgrace the royal family by his plans to exploit
Silviane sexually.

But when Mérovée dies, ultimate power falls to
Childéric, who, in a confusion of political and sexual
roles seeks to double the king's absolute control. On a
pretext, he removes Andrimarte from the court, believing
that now he will be able to pursue freely Silviane. The
young woman lives in the greatest apprehension and fear
during the absence of her husband. Completely defense-
less, she seeks to protect herself from the prince's wild
aggression. She vows suicide, but in a move toward self-
preservation, she decides to cut off her hair and dress
up as a boy, fleeing seconds before the arrival of
Childéric.

The new king's people, however, can no longer bear his
preoccupation with sex, nor his "mollesses efféminées,"
which detract from his ability to wage war on behalf of
the kingdom. In his lustful excess, he is carrying along
with him many of the region's young men. Both Franks and

Gauls rebel against this reign of debauchery and violence; Childéric is forced to flee. And ultimately (but not before part 5), Andrimarte and Silviane are reunited. ALCIDON, DAPHNIDE, AND EURIC. This tale offers a "twist": while Daphnide, the heroine, is the conventional beauty of d'Urfé's novel, and loves a young chevalier, Alcidon, she is also ambitious. But the narrative is particularly difficult to follow; its center disappears, as names wildly proliferate, leading us in a web of greater and greater disorientation. What does clearly emerge, however, from this tale gone haywire is a nightmare of deception and deceit.

The story, highly romanesque, is curious from the beginning. Alcidon is a knight in the service of Euric, king of the Visigoths. A fine soldier, his mind is nonetheless continually preoccupied with Daphnide. While fighting in Provence, he is able to arrange a clandestine meeting with her at L'Isle de Sorgues. Upon arriving at the residence where Daphnide is awaiting him, Alcidon finds at the door a mythical Diane-type figure named Délie (this being, in fact, one of the goddess's other names), seminude, who is supposedly Daphnide's sister. Page after page of the narrative describes the minutes that Alcidon and Daphnide spend together, even those in bed, but where Délie is also present, thus blocking satisfaction! The tone here is decidedly teasing, but with the beginning of King Euric's insatiable curiosity to learn the details of Alcidon's adventures with Daphnide, the thrust of the narrative shifts to a more menacing tone. Male aggression is again the problem, as Euric abandons war pursuits for those of hunting and love adventures.

Learning of Euric's passion for Daphnide, Alcidon experiences a strong sense of betrayal by the very man he had labored to serve. He becomes violently jealous, although his insecurity is based primarily on a mere rumor of Daphnide's infidelity. Alcidon's depression brings him close to death, and Daphnide, who is now living at the court, must explain to him why she has decided to receive Euric. Her decision, she says, is essentially political: by allowing the king to visit her, she will ensure remaining at the court, thereby continuing to be close to Alcidon.

Her ruse is complex. Not only must she pretend interest in Euric; she also wishes for Alcidon to feign love for a certain Clarinte, another of the king's women, and

who, she fears, will one day obtain enough power to
banish both Daphnide and Alcidon. Situationally, this
sham duplicates that arranged by Astrée between Céladon
and Aminthe, and although in both cases intentions are
good, results are typically disastrous. Even though
Daphnide herself, like Astrée, concocted the pretend
romance, she quickly becomes suspicious, fearing that
Alcidon is no longer merely feigning interest in
Clarinte.

Ultimately, Euric decides to wed Daphnide. Her reaction to this proposal is ambiguous, and Alcidon accuses
her of sheer ambition in accepting him. There is truth
to the accusation. What Daphnide seems to have sought
was both an assured position as queen, and Alcidon, as
well, although not as a husband. She comes up short,
however, for Euric dies before a wedding can occur. The
unhappy tale concludes only in Forez where an oracle has
sent Daphnide and Alcidon, and where, in the end, they
are reunited by Adamas. They also don pastoral habits,
thereby renouncing their former status, and "bending
their spirit to the gentle, naive world of shepherds and
their innocent games" [3:497].

DORINDE, SIGISMOND, AND GONDEBAUD. When Dorinde first
arrives in Forez, she is the enigmatic stranger who hates
men: "All men deceive . . . and the most faithful one
resembles the chameleon who changes color according to
the objects it touches" [4:164]. Given her story, this
opinion is hardly surprising. Unusually beautiful,
Dorinde was sought after by many men. She was engaged to
Periandre, but he abandons her after an illness leaves
her face scarred. Another suitor, Merindor, continues to
love her even though she is no longer beautiful, but her
father forces an engagement with Bellimarte. Unfortunately, as matters turn out, Bellimarte is already married!
Thus, not surprisingly, Dorinde comes to distrust men.

Her face eventually heals, and Gondebaud requests that
she come serve the princess Clothilde. Gondebaud himself
now desires her, but suspicion of all males makes her
wary. In order to achieve his goals, Gondebaud has his
aide, Ardilan, pretend to woo Dorinde's lady, Darinée,
thereby hoping to gain easier access to Dorinde's heart.

When Gondebaud's son, Sigismond, learns of his
father's passion for Dorinde, he, too, begins to covet
her. The young woman reciprocates his interest, but she
harbors a secret ambition to be queen, and thus continues
to allow Gondebaud to woo her. (She later admits to

having been foolish and wonders how she could have allowed herself to believe Gondebaud's vague promises.) Ultimately, however, a real mutual love develops between Sigismond and Dorinde. The former seems genuinely involved, no longer merely a rival to his father. But the relationship between father and son is violent. When Gondebaud learns of Sigismond's feelings for Dorinde, he becomes enraged; the son, in turn, openly rebels against his father. (This occurs in part 4, where such revolts are common.)

Sigismond and Dorinde then plan to flee together. At the appointed time and place, Dorinde waits, but Sigismond fails to arrive. Believing she has once again been duped, Dorinde departs on foot, alone. In reality, Sigismond's plan has been discovered by his father, who had the gates to the city locked. But Dorinde, bitter and afraid, is now on her own, and she arrives in Forez only because of the protection offered her by an old man.

Gondebaud then sends his men to capture Dorinde, but she is saved by the good efforts of Godomar, Sigismond's brother, and, paradoxically, by her former admirers, Periandre and Merindor, who accompanied Godomar, and who are now sworn to protect Dorinde. Sigismond, however, is unable to escape from his father who joins forces with Polémas in an effort to destroy Marcilly, where Dorinde now resides, protected by Amasis. After Polémas's defeat and death, Sigismond determines to calm his father's ire; in this he is successful, and, aided by the princess Clothilde, obtains from Gondebaud acceptance of his marriage to Dorinde.

Conclusion

The eight "secondary" tales described in the preceding pages are not necessarily familiar ones. The excerpted version of L'Astrée most commonly read today is the "10/18" pocket edition, which includes only the Astrée-Céladon romance. While almost all the themes d'Urfé sought to convey are developed in that tale, such a presentation inevitably falsifies the nature of the book. Because of space limitations, only brief summaries of the so-called secondary tales can be offered, yet many of them are as long as the Astrée-Céladon narrative, which itself occupies a small portion of the complete novel.

If, however, the reader is familiar with these sto-

ries, he or she will doubtless appreciate how falsifying
it ultimately is to attempt such cursory rehashes. Most
of the tales span books and volumes, and the brevity of
the summary form denies them their majestic scope.
Indeed, for the modern reader, well versed or not in
L'Astrée, the stories described in this chapter may
seem convoluted, artificial, even silly. Without the
"pull" of d'Urfé's prose, the narratives appear trite,
lacking true drama. Such is not the case when one examines closely the original text. In almost all instances,
these tales are the best part of reading d'Urfé's novel,
for they are charged with all the necessary ingredients
of good romance: sex, violence, and generational con-
flicts. One can only hope that the summaries provided
here will encourage further reading of the original text,
and not merely serve to replace it!

Apart from the need to transcend the principal stories, there is another reason for proposing these summaries of several secondary tales. Paradoxically, to
elucidate distinction in this instance is the best means
to allow for the striking sameness of the component parts
to emerge. It is difficult to recall readily the specif-
ics of Alcidon and Daphnide's story or to distinguish its
details from the story of Cryséide and Arimant. D'Urfé
does little in his novel to achieve a strong sense of
differential distinction, of characterization. While the
experience of reading one of these tales is totally
encompassing and engrossing, it is easy to forget "what
happened." The reader's faulty memory is not a result of
the novel's length. Rather, the problem is that Honoré
d'Urfé has created a universe where distinction fades in
favor of a blur of repeating patterns.

The names alone are strikingly similar. There are
Silvie and Silviane; Childéric and Euric; Ligdamon and
Lydias—and each of the pair plays a role not too different from the other. Dorinde and her confidante,
Darinée, are both tricked by men. Even gender distinctions are blurred. Damon's lover, Madonte, enjoys a name
composed of virtually the same letters as his own. For
ultimately, there are no differences, not from story to
story, hero to hero, villain to villain, or man to woman.
The non-French, Greek sounding names are a trap. Designed to convey unicity, they succeed only in creating a
nonreferential world where character fades in favor of
the same obsessive theme of passion (3). D'Urfé's stories may be indistinguishable, even monotonous, in their

basic format.   But taken together, they form an incredi-
ble literary fresco, where monotony is rapidly transformed into an awareness of the obsessive nature of human
loving.   L'Astrée is as "monotonous" as Proust's A La
Recherche du temps perdu or as the letters of Mme de
Sévigné.   In each case, repetition within an exterior
framework of distinction—a different character, a different letter—is the means to communicate the essential
sameness of the human predicament.

Chapter Four
Half the Story:
The Philosophical Claims

At the base of L'Astrée is a conception of love which
the novel's philosopher-intellectuals, Adamas and
Silvandre, regularly articulate. They are usually found
discoursing—preaching, lecturing, judging, debating—in
a massively verbose effort to formulate a code of loving
that combines principles inherited from medieval "courtoisie" with those of Renaissance Platonism. The result is
a highly spiritualized portrait of love, so abstract that
it "functions" only within a verbal format. Left to
become "act," this love flounders, as it meets, head on,
more realistic needs.

The philosophically oriented passages of the novel,
however, occupy many pages, and over the years they have
come to be the principal focus for many d'Urfé scholars.
Why this should be is not entirely clear. The Renaissance era was split by two conceptions of love: on the
one hand, Platonic spiritualism, and, on the other, a
more realistic appreciation of human desire. The shift
toward a less lofty description of love was a European-
wide phenomenon. Viewed in this light, L'Astrée,
which offers both spiritualism and its negation, would
therefore be the culmination of an age's intellectual
journey.

Why, then, do so many still cling to the view that
d'Urfé's novel is a vehicle for exposing Renaissance
Platonic thought? Perhaps because of what occurs,
critically, when a writer pursues both nonfiction and
fiction. We often look to the fictional work to embody
the ideas expressed in the essays. For Honoré d'Urfé's
work, such a link is all too readily assumed. The
Epistres Morales clearly stress the concepts of Renaissance Platonism, and thus L'Astrée, too, it is determined, seeks to deliver the same "message."

But the ultimate reason for such an interpretation
goes beyond L'Astrée, perhaps, to a general view of
literature as a teacher of moral principles. Northrop
Frye has addressed this issue in The Secular Scripture,
and his analysis accurately describes the critical situa-

tion which has befallen L'Astrée: "In every age it
has been generally assumed that the function of serious
literature is to produce illustrations of the higher
truths conveyed by expository prose. The real social
function of literature, in this view, is to persuade the
emotions to align themselves with the reason. . . . The
disputes are mainly, not about the status of literature,
but about how efficient the serious aspect of serious
literature is in separating itself from the moral turpi-
tude of mere entertainment" (1). In this view, the
efforts of scholars to portray the spiritual views of
Silvandre and Adamas as the true center of the novel, and
more, as the true beliefs of Honoré d'Urfé, would be
the result of this critical need to establish the supremacy of reason, and, subsequently, of "serious" literature.

But what of the "other" L'Astrée? The novel is
hardly an exclusive dissertation on the value of spiritual love. Vast numbers of pages in this immense book are
devoted to the "realistic" portrait of love, to a far
less elevated picture than that painted by Adamas. Such
"realistic" passages are, to follow Frye's analysis, both
morally questionable and highly entertaining. Aside from
the preachy discoursing of Hylas—which matches in form
at least the long-winded exposés of the novel's Neoplatonic thinkers—these sections form the "action" center
of L'Astrée, interrupting, often explosively, the
expository text. Sexually titillating for both characters and readers, these "act" oriented sections contrast
dramatically with the passages where characters posit,
judge, explain, debate, or interpret. In short, these
parts are fun to read, good entertainment, solid romance.
But they are more than all that, for while the preaching
of an Adamas or a Silvandre lauds reason as the basis for
all of human behavior, many of the "action" passages
depict the opposite: man (and woman) under the sway of
powerful emotions, and not guided at all by the firm hand
of reason. The social function of literature alluded to
by Frye, as a purveyor of "higher" moral positions, is
persistently undermined in L'Astrée.

The present volume is an attempt to explore the dual
nature of love in d'Urfé's novel. If many scholars have
persisted in conveying that the novel's "heart" is the
spiritual love advocated by Silvandre and Adamas, more
recently others have focused on the overt and covert
sexual aspects of d'Urfé's work. Most notable is
Gérard Genette's essay, "Le Serpent dans la Bergerie,"

the title of which alone suggests a phallic intrusion
into pastoral bliss. Both approaches overstate their
case. In L'Astrée, two worlds coexist, negating, but
thereby correcting, each other, prohibiting undue emphasis on either the soul or the body. These two domains
are, moreover, distinguished not only thematically, but
also structurally. The description of spiritual love
remains on the level of discourse, while the erotic is
most often shown as "act" (through, of course, the medium
of language). This chapter will highlight the network of
metaphysical beliefs which together produce the spiritualized portrait of love, while later sections will concentrate on how Honoré d'Urfé systematically contradicts
this philosophical base, so deeply rooted in Occidental
thought.

The Historical Context

Henri IV's reign ws marked by an effort to purify both
sexual customs and language. This struggle against
libertine influences was, not surprisingly, encouraged by
aristocratic women who, seeking a more dignified treat-
ment of the female, naturally turned to the ideals posed
by medieval "courtoisie." Moreover, for cultivated
French society these values, with their emphasis on
respect for women, had never entirely lost their force.
Despite libertine tendencies in the society at large, the
"courtois" message of deference still held appeal for
many sixteenth-century readers (2). This body of literature, portraying knights in service to their "dame," had
established a code of behavior necessary for loving in a
societal situation that demanded the utmost discretion.
The "perfect" lover, always respectful of his mistress,
continually bowed to her wishes, while remaining loyal
and faithful to her. Violations to this fundamental code
were met with severe punishment and bans.
    In composing L'Astrée, d'Urfé was strongly influ-
enced by the ideals of the "courtois" tradition. There
is, however, one significant difference: rarely are the
relationships in L'Astrée adulterous. Pastoral literature required a more "naive" presentation of sexual
behavior, and idyllic innocence, at least on the surface,
is one of the genre's primary conventions. But the
pastoral mode was also a useful one for d'Urfé, who,

through the manipulation of narrative techniques, was able to convey a highly charged, if usually covert, erotic atmosphere. This difference aside—and it is substantial—d'Urfé echoed the basic concepts of "courtois" literature, all centering on male submissiveness to the demands of a lady.

These conventions meshed harmoniously with the fundamental tenets of Renaissance Platonism, which more than any other body of thought, governs the "high" tone of L'Astrée. According to this analysis, true love is always spiritual, rather than physical, and it is therefore based on inner beauty and goodness and guided by the principle of reason. The Platonic mode so apparent in Epistres Morales and L'Astrée reflected the thinking of Italian writers, and in particular that of Marsilio Ficino, Pico della Mirandola, Pietro Bembo, Mario Equicola, and Leone Ebreo. It was principally Ficino who, in his Commentary on Plato's Symposium, laid the most substantial foundation for the French Renaissance writers, including d'Urfé. Ficino's work was translated into French four times during the sixteenth century; its appeal and influence on Italian and French intellectuals were preeminent.

Ficino offered a strong, positive view of women, who, in the Platonic tradition, are viewed as superior beings, the terrestrial link to God. Most significantly for d'Urfé, Ficino's work elaborated a philosophy of love as a source of all good, and of beauty as the reflection of that inner good. His writings, along with those of his fellow Italians and of the French Renaissance Platonists as well, theorized the origin of love, described the transformation of true lovers' souls, and postulated a belief in eternal happiness for those who love mutually and perfectly. These works also formulated a strong connection between human and divine love, a concept which d'Urfé explored in the Epistres Morales, if considerably less in L'Astrée (3). To approach these diverse notions as they relate to L'Astrée, and for the purpose of clarity, I have divided them into subdivisions. I hope it will be quickly understood, however, that these concepts are closely related and flow one into the other. What will emerge is a picture of a highly intellectualized form of love, whereby the erotic is effectively denied and ultimately effaced.

Modes of "Courtoisie" in *L'Astrée*

While in L'Astrée, d'Urfé rejected the "courtois"
convention of adultery, he carefully preserved the fundamental ideas of discretion, fidelity, and obedience on
the part of the male admirer. The men make valiant
efforts to adhere to the "courtois" code, which exerts a
powerful sense of control over them. As the principal
masculine figures, both Céladon and Silvandre attempt to
live by the precepts of chivalry which social and literary tradition had established for them. They, and various secondary figures as well, try to conform to a rigid
pattern of behavior founded on ultimate fidelity and
submission.

The expectation is to achieve the status of "le parfait amant," the perfect lover, who not only is discreet
in his amorous entanglements, thereby preserving the
honor and reputation of his "lady," but who also is
unswerving in devotion, faithful in practice, and obedi-
ent to all her commands. In short, the lover's every
effort must be toward complying with the social and
psychological demands imposed on him by a woman, whose
needs are secrecy, loyalty, and chastity. "CELER ET
TAIRE" [2:454]—"to conceal and be silent"—says
Léonide, is a fundamental love commandment. Almost all
the female characters in L'Astrée are obsessed with
the imperative for secrecy. The greatest threat to their
reputation appears to lie in the public discovery that
they love, or even, that they are loved. No action that
might destroy their honor need occur; it is sufficient
that the world knows they love for a soiled reputation to
be born. Even the high and the mighty, the characters of
rank, are wary of public opinion. Galathée, in the
interests of preserving her reputation, makes every
effort to conceal Céladon's presence in her castle,
except from those closest to her. Other women experience
so strong a fear of public discovery that they risk
destroying their only chance for happiness. Silvie's
obsessive anxiety is that the world will detect
Ligdamon's feelings for her; thus, she bans him from any
commerce with her. It is also, of course, this fear of
public condemnation that leads Céladon and Astrée to
the subterfuge which is the cause of their many problems.
But theory and practice rarely mesh in L'Astrée, and
it is the former, based on the traditional concepts

culled from "courtois" literature that posits the wisdom
of ultimate discretion.

It is equally important that the law of total fidelity
be maintained. Absolute faithfulness is perhaps the most
significant service that the perfect lover can render to
his beloved. On one level, it assures the woman's psychological tranquillity. But this is far from the whole
story. According to Silvandre, fidelity is the essence
of the entire relationship, for it alone establishes the
transcendental nature of perfect spiritual love. Unable
to consummate the relationship until marriage, the lover
must nonetheless never seek carnal satisfaction with
another. For Hylas, who finds such a philosophy depress-
ing in its negation of human drives, Silvandre formulates
an elaborate reply:

> If you were capable of understanding, you wouldn't
> ask me, as you do, what the rewards are for these
> faithful lovers you call mournful and pensive. You
> would realize that they are thrilled to contemplate
> the treasure they adore, and that, scornful of every-
> thing in the world, there is nothing that bothers them
> more than the loss of time they are forced to spend
> elsewhere. . . . And you should know that the reward
> love extends to faithful lovers is the very same as to
> the gods, and to those men who, transcending human na-
> ture, rise almost to the level of the divinities.
> [2:389]

The sublime nature of a wholly faithful love, according to Silvandre, is not only a means to transcend the
limited life of the physical senses. To live contrary to
the principles of fidelity is to negate the very essence
of love, which the young philosopher perceives as indivis-
ible: "Love is not love as soon as the smallest element
separates itself . . . for if affection lacks the least
particle, such feeling is no more part of love than cold
is part of heat, and if fidelity is absent from strong
affection, it is betrayal, not love. If fidelity is first
there, but is not permanent, not everlasting, it is not
fidelity, but perfidy" [2:381-82]. It is this rigid
principle to which Céladon will try to adhere throughout
L'Astrée, rejecting, for example, the advances of
Galathée and Léonide, or the temptation of Silvie, in
order to remain perfectly faithful to Astrée. Other
characters, equally inflexible, interpret the notion of

constancy and loyalty as extending beyond the grave.
Thus, Diane vows unending fidelity to Filandre as he lays
dying; and Tircis will love no other than Cléon, even
after her death. The strict notion of faithfulness is a major tenet of
L'Astrée's philosophical base, and joins that of absolute obedience to the female. This principle is a sign
of the male's respect for the woman he loves, and submission to her is the guiding principle of his behavior. In
L'Astrée, such obedience occurs both when the characters are "sincere" (as is the case of Céladon and
Astrée); when they are pretending (as when Silvandre and
Phillis, on a wager, rival to serve best their "mistress," Diane); and when they are disguised (thus,
"Alexis" seeks to establish himself as servant to his
mistress, Astrée). Obedience is the hallmark of the
code by which the characters aspire to live, even to the
point of total self-abnegation.
So it is that Adamas cannot persuade Céladon to
appear before Astrée once she has banished him from her
sight. The dialogue between the two men reflects
Céladon's effort to live the letter of her law:

> I'll think, said Adamas, that you really don't love
> Astrée, if knowing that she loves you, and consider-
> ing that you are free to see her, you still keep your
> distance.
>
> Love, said the shepherd, prohibits me from disobeying
> her. And since she ordered me not to show myself, can
> you call it a breach of love if I observe her order?
>
> When she so ordered, spoke the druid, she hated you.
> But at this moment, she loves you and weeps for you
> not as someone who's absent, but as someone who's
> dead.
>
> Whatever the situation may be, replied Céladon, she
> ordered it, and . . . I wish to obey her. [2:396]

Adamas's words make good sense. He suggests that Astrée
no longer feels anger toward Céladon, having discovered
her error in judgment, and he therefore urges Céladon to
appear before her. Céladon recognizes the commonsense
approach of Adamas, but his eagerness to abide by the
letter of the "courtois" code determines and molds his

conduct. The result of his effort is not only a prolonga-
tion of the novel, but also the hero's extreme sense of
alienation. The code, however, as interpreted by
d'Urfé's characters, demands this total obedience. And
it is only through a form of subterfuge that Céladon
will finally break that code, allowing him to adhere to
the letter of the law, while brazenly violating its
spirit.

Platonic Love Doctrines in *L'Astrée*—The Religion of Love

The "courtois" tradition ultimately blends in L'Astrée with the dominant Neoplatonic model to form a
general concept of love as a spiritual experience, so
abstractly conceived that a modern reader's mind may
frequently wander. We are no longer accustomed to thinking of human desire along religious or mythical grounds,
having replaced such terminology with Freudian and post-
Freudian vocabulary. For earlier thinkers, however, love
was perceived as a great divinity, the oldest of the
gods. D'Urfé portrays him as the same Tautates, who
reigns supreme in the druidic faith. The characters in
L'Astrée all refer to the love deity as an extraordinary power, a total presence, whose domination is univer-
sal. There is a strong effort on d'Urfé's part to
reconcile Platonic thought with Christian faith; hence,
reflecting the Christian belief in God as a form of love,
Tautates and Love become, in L'Astrée, one and the
same. Having established this relationship, however,
d'Urfé is still able to maintain his central focus on
the omnipotence of love. As the words of Tircis show, in
Forez love is perceived as an absolute: "Love . . . is
so great a god, that it desires nothing outside itself:
it is its own center, and has no purpose that does not
begin and end with itself" [2:262-63].
The image of love as an omnipotent deity, independent
of any mediating influence, is maintained throughout
L'Astrée. Even when overt religious terminology is
absent, the reader detects a strong sense of ultimate
authority, which sometimes capriciously sanctions behavior contrary to societal norms. When Galathée asks
Léonide if love is not dependent on the laws of virtue,
the nymph replies that "Love . . . is something greater

than virtue . . . and formulates its own set of laws,
without seeking any help" [1:343]. There is an ambiva-
lence in L'Astrée, however. While in some instances,
d'Urfé ties love to a Christian-type deity, at other
moments what emerges is more the sense of a despotic
tyrant, whose control is independent of traditional Christian concepts. But whichever direction surfaces at a
given moment, the picture remains essentially one of
total power: the true, and only, god of L'Astrée is
love.

LOVE, BEAUTY, AND GOODNESS. In the Epistres
Morales, d'Urfé had shown how love is a desire for
beauty. His arguments faithfully followed the Renaissance Platonists, for whom beauty, goodness, and love
were intertwined and inseparable. But in this perspective, beauty has a special significance: the physical
loveliness of a human being is a reflection of God's
unique beauty, which in turn is the essence of all good.
When, therefore, one loves and desires a beautiful
person, he is craving the ultimate source of goodness,
the ultimate principle of happiness, the divine spirit.
It is quite naturally Adamas, the druidic priest and wise
man, who is called on to explain to Céladon the binding
relationship among God, beauty, and love: "You must
understand that all beauty has its origin in the supreme
goodness we call God, and that it [beauty] is a beam of
light he projects on all things he has created" [2:78].
As Maxime Gaume has shown, Adamas's views are a simplifi-
cation of ideas far more elaborately expressed by the
Italian Renaissance Platonists (4). D'Urfé never wished
to utilize in his novel the subtle intricacies of Platonic thought; his efforts were toward conveying the
association between creature and divine beauty, in a
format acceptable for a novel. While simplified, however, the precepts follow carefully the fundamental
elements of Renaissance Platonism.

Beauty has its origin in God, who is the essence of
all good. Thus love, which is the desire for beauty, must
always reflect this goodness. But what exactly is this
beauty, and how is it perceived? In the Platonic view,
beauty of the soul is of particular value, transcending
the limited duration of physical attractiveness and
thereby of love based exclusively on the senses. This is
precisely what Célidée understood when she ravaged her
face with a diamond, so as to leave permanent scars. She
was determined to learn if either Thamire or Calidon

would remain faithful to her once she no longer possessed her superior beauty: "Let me make myself appear as I wish to be accepted. My beauty is cause for Calidon to forget his sense of duty [to Thamire], and for Thamire himself to neglect his own health; . . . thus, by the loss of something as fleeting as physical beauty, we will all be able henceforth to live in freedom, removed from this obsessive worry" [2:448]. By disfiguring herself, Célidée hopes to force the world to see beyond her outer beauty to the inner superiority she prizes above all else. Calidon, of course, fails the test; but Thamire is able to transcend limited notions of corporal attraction to value Célidée's true worth.

If beauty must be prized, first, as a special characteristic of the soul, and, second, of the body, then it must be revealed by diverse means: principally through sight, hearing, and understanding or judgment. For iconoclastic Hylas, who is moved exclusively by evident physical beauty, sight alone is sufficient for him to become enamored, but Silvandre repeatedly explains that this sense is not sufficient for a love relationship. It is not that Silvandre completely rejects the notion of physical attraction; rather, he seeks to persuade that it is ephemeral in comparison with the lasting beauty of the soul. The latter, of course, cannot be perceived by the eyes, but is wholly conveyed through the power of sound judgment: "Certainly, it is first our eyes which allow love to penetrate our hearts. . . . The eyes, thus, may ignite and fan a new attraction, but when this feeling is assured, it needs more firmness, something more solid, to make it perfect, and that can only be knowledge of virtue, beauty, and merit, along with the mutual affection of she whom we love" [2:13]. In this highly civilized picture that Silvandre paints, carnal desire has been so tamed that it cannot interfere with the rarified atmosphere of spiritual love.

LOVE, KNOWLEDGE, AND REASON. The passage from Frye's The Secular Scripture cited earlier gives an excellent summary of how "serious" literature is envisaged in a world perceived as "civilized." The emotions are to be portrayed as aligned with reason. In this regard, Honoré d'Urfé faithfully adheres to a basic premise of rational control over passion. D'Urfé, like many of his generation, was marked by the principles of neo-Stoicism, which stressed reliance on an energetic reason and will to combat the enervating emotions. The self is affirmed

in a proud battle against human appetites, seen as
inherently animalistic and degrading. To Hylas, the
strongest supporter in L'Astrée of passionate, sensual
love, Silvandre extols the supremacy of reason: "Those
other pleasures which are so important to you, are only
those which a bastard love gives to unreasoning animals,
and to those men who, degrading themselves below the
level of human nature, themselves become almost animals,
deprived of all reason. And it is to the level of a
monster, Hylas, that you degenerate, when you love other
than as you should. . . . On the other hand, my love is
so perfect that nothing may be added to or subtracted
from it without offending reason" [2:389]. Célidée,
too, had referred to Thamire and Calidon as "monsters,"
for their voracious desire. (Moreover, this battle
between reason and the "monsters" will go on throughout
the seventeenth century, whose writers found in the beast
terminology a successful metaphor for the irrational
passions.)

In the Platonic tradition, love is the most desired
goal of all, so long as it is "reasonable." To achieve
such status, it must be based on more than superficial
attraction. It is the role of reason to recognize the
good that provokes a loving feeling, but such goodness
may only be perceived through knowledge of merit and
virtue. Hylas and Silvandre frequently debate this
point, Silvandre maintaining that love comes only with
deep familiarity, while Hylas reveals that he has always
loved successfully without such knowledge. Silvandre
agrees that we may initially be seduced by a pretty face
(and thus the reference to the importance of the eyes),
but true love will always be founded on an awareness of
inner goodness and beauty.

THE ORIGIN OF LOVE: "SYMPATHIE" AND MAGNETIC
ATTRACTION. That reason and knowledge are the guiding
principles of an enduring love is a familiar precept of
Platonic thought. But what, precisely, is the origin of
love? This question preoccupied Renaissance Platonists,
and d'Urfé as well. To state that love depends on seeing is only to establish the means by which we find ourselves in a love situation. But such a conclusion does
not explain why one person comes to love another. Something other than perceived beauty must be involved, for
even the most strikingly beautiful person is not loved by
all! Rather, love, in the Platonic view, is predestined.
Whom we love is a result not of free choice, but of a

mysterious "sympathie" which ultimately determines what
we like to believe is a spontaneous reaction.

It falls to Adamas, once more, to articulate the notion of preordained partners. In formulating this theory,
Honoré d'Urfé was probably inspired by Ficino, although
in L'Astrée the concepts appear in a vastly simplified
form. Two people who love each other are similar in
their fundamental identity. "Sympathie," then, "is this
identity we find in one another," and it, in turn, "is
the true source of love." Adamas continues: "if beauty
were the source of love, it would follow that all beautiful people were loved by everyone. But it is often the
opposite: we see that the most beautiful and worthy are
not the most agreeable to us, but rather that we love
best those who are most like us" [3:264]. The underlying
factor determining such a powerful attraction, as interpreted by Ficino and subsequently by d'Urfé, is plane-
tary. It is the beauty of a certain planet that radiates
from the self and which determines who will attract us.

This theory, loosely constructed from Plato's Symposium, is elaborated by Honoré d'Urfé in yet another
fashion, which maintains the twin concepts of "sympathie"
and predestination in love matters. The myth of magnetic
attraction became for the author of L'Astrée a potent
and tangible means to express Platonic philosophy on the
origin of love. It is difficult to determine the precise
source for this formulation of love as a type of magnetism. Maxime Gaume has shown how much the sixteenth-
century mind was fascinated by the concept of magnetic
pull. But he also suggests that the notion of the
magnetic stone as described by Plato may also have
influenced d'Urfé (5).

It is Céladon who describes (rather vaguely, it must
be said) how magnetism functions in the world of spiritual love, although the ideas he expresses are those of
Silvandre. The latter, "when asked why he doesn't love
anyone, replies that he hasn't found his magnet, but that
when he does locate it, he knows that inevitably he will
fall in love just like everyone else" [1:387]. Céladon
explains that Silvandre's theory is guided by the presumption that "when God created all our souls, men and women
alike, he touched each with a magnet" [1:387]. Next, he
placed the men's and women's souls in separate locations.
When eventually he coordinated souls with human forms,
he took the women's souls to the place where are the
magnetic pieces that touched the men's souls, while the

latter are led to where the stones are that had touched
the women's souls. Each soul selects a magnetic stone.
The result is that when one person meets another who has
his or her magnetic piece, it is inevitable that these
two must fall in love.
Those who are gathered around Céladon to hear him
explain Silvandre's ideas are initially skeptical. They
have several questions for him. Why, for example, will
one shepherd love several shepherdesses? Céladon's
reply is ingenious: the magnet that touched the shepherd's soul broke into several pieces, and therefore
several women all have a portion. He will naturally be
attracted to them all. The group also ponders the matter
of the "âmes larronnesses," the robber souls, who
grabbed more magnets than was their due. Now possessing
several, they have deprived other souls, who are left, so
to speak, empty-handed. Then someone wishes to know why,
after "having loved someone a very long time, it is possible to leave her for someone else" [1:388]. Again, the
solution is ingenious: both those who are loved possess
a piece of the same magnetic stone, and the lover was
simply attracted first to the person who had the larger
share, then, later, to the one with the smaller piece.
    The theory of magnetism was a more tangible way for
d'Urfé to explain the fundamental Platonic theory of
"sympathie." He was obviously more comfortable with it
than with the subtleties of the Renaissance Platonists,
which were cumbersome in a fictional work. All such
expressions of predestined love, however, imply a level
of determinism at odds with the belief in the power of
reason to guide human choice. It would seem, therefore,
that while d'Urfé evoked an initial attraction which is
predetermined and thus beyond the rational level, subsequently he suggests that love must be founded on a base
of reason and free will.
    TRANSFORMATION THROUGH SPIRITUAL UNION. One of the
most fundamental tenets of Platonic thought is that there
is a fusion, a union between two loving souls, such that
the two become fundamentally one. For Plato, true love
was viewed as always mutual, and the Renaissance Platonists (both the Italian essayists and the French poets
who were influenced by them) utilized this basic premise
to formulate the perfectability of reciprocal affection.
In L'Astrée, Honoré d'Urfé writes that this mutual
feeling leads to the couple's ultimate union, in a
transcendence achieved through perfect spiritual love.

Unlike other Renaissance thinkers, however, d'Urfé suggests no ultimate union with God. L'Astrée remains a secular work; its god is love, but a human, terrestrial love, whose link with the deity is considerably more remote than that envisioned by true Platonists. Leaving aside this distinction, however, d'Urfé's thought follows faithfully the fundamental Platonic concept of the joining of two souls. One of the earliest substories of L'Astrée, that of Damon and Fortune (based entirely on paintings depicting this romance and narrated by Adamas), utilizes myth to convey the law of mutual love. Adamas is describing the second painting in the series to his auditors. He urges them to "look over here, and observe this Anteros who, with chains of roses and flowers, is tying the arms and neck of the beautiful shepherdess Fortune, and who then brings her over to the shepherd [Damon]: this is to convey that the merit, love, and service of this handsome shepherd, which are represented by the flowers, obligate Fortune to love him as he loves her" [1:444]. Such perfect harmony is expressed elsewhere in the novel by Silvandre, who describes a painting in the temple of Astrée. Silvandre's narration focuses on the intertwining of two love figures, represented by the linking of their bows and the exchange of their arrows. The flames from their torches intermingle. Silvandre concludes that "by this joining of bows and flames, and by this exchange of arrows," one can perceive "the union of two wills into one, and . . . that the Lover and the Beloved are one" [2:180].

The realization of this almost mystical union, as expressed by d'Urfé, may occur only if the lover is willing to submit totally to the wishes of his mistress. The self fades in favor of this transcendental bonding, and the lover spiritually becomes the beloved. This transformation of the soul, implying complete self-abnegation, is at the heart of Renaissance Platonic thought, and d'Urfé extends it, as did the Italian writers, to the concept of death of the self. Discoursing with Hylas, Silvandre rhetorically queries: "Do you know what it means to love?" And then supplies the answer himself: "The self dies and is reborn spiritually in the Other" [1:290]. This theme spans d'Urfé's novel, and it is frequently the subject of the book's many poems and letters. One sonnet, linking Eros and Thanetos, describes how the love wish and death wish become one and the same: "Pour revivre en autrui vouloir mourir en soi"

("To live as the other, wish one's self to die") [3:565].
This transformation of the Self into the spirit of the
Other is the last major tenet of Renaissance Platonism
that interested the author of L'Astrée. In his novel,
d'Urfé orchestrated the principles of Platonic and "courtois" thinking into a veritable hymn of spiritual love,
nowhere more evident than in his Twelve Tables of the
Laws of Love.

The Twelve Tables of the Laws of Love

The Twelve Tables (part 2), a masterful testimony to
the ideals expressed in L'Astrée, are inscribed at the
bottom of the painting in Astrée's temple, the same
painting that served to depict the fundamental unity of
two loving souls. The laws are inviolable: every lover
who wishes to avoid disgrace must observe them. To the
assembled group of "bergers" and "bergères" who find
themselves at the temple, Silvandre reads aloud the
Twelve Tables. They are included here because they beau-
tifully convey the essence of pastoral Platonism, and
because they so stunningly are parodied by Hylas (as
shown in chapter 5), in his effort to alter the abstract
principles which he finds ludicrous for daily existence.
Silvandre, on the other hand, cannot read the Tables with
enough admiration:

The First Table

Qui veut être parfait amant,
Il faut qu'il aime infiniment:
L'extrême amour seul en est digne,
Aussi la médiocrité,
De trahison est plutôt signe,
Que non pas de fidélité.

He who wishes to be the perfect lover,
Must love infinitely: Only sublime love
    is worthy,
Thus a mediocre love
Is more a sign of betrayal
Than of faithfulness.

Having thus established the "courtois" ideal of "the

perfect lover," d'Urfé moves on to the Platonic belief
of love as a divinity:

The Second Table

Qu'il n'aime jamais qu'en un lieu,
Et que cet amour soit un dieu,
Qu'il adore pour toute chose:
Et n'ayant jamais qu'un objet,
Tous les bonheurs qu'il se propose,
Soient pour cet unique sujet.

May he love in one place alone,
And may this love be for him a god,
Whom he adores for every thing:
And having only one object,
Let all the happiness he desires
Be for this unique subject.

D'Urfé's poetry is at its best in these Twelve Tables.
The second table plays with words to establish an identity between "objet" and "sujet" that convey the totality
of the beloved's supremacy and control.

The Third Table

Bornant en lui tous ses plaisirs,
Qu'il arrête tous ses désirs
Au service de cette belle,
Voire qu'il cesse de s'aimer,
Sinon que d'autant qu'aimé d'elle,
Il se doit pour elle estimer.

Limiting all his pleasures,
May he have no wishes
Other than service to this beauty,
Indeed may he quit loving himself,
Except insofar as loved by her,
He owes himself respect.

The above table begins the principle of self-abnegation
dear to both medieval "courtois" idealists and to Renaissance Platonists, which by table 8, will have extended
to spiritual death of the self. It also concentrates
on the word "service," thereby establishing yet again

the nature of the "courtois" relationship.

The Fourth Table

Que s'il a le soin d'être mieux,
Ce ne soit que pour les beaux yeux
Dont son amour a pris naissance.
S'il souhaite plus de bonheur,
Ce ne soit que pour l'espérance
Qu'elle en recevra plus d'honneur.

If he desires to improve himself,
Let it be only for the beautiful eyes
From which his love sprung.
If he seeks greater happiness,
Let it be only in the hope
That she will thus receive greater honor.

The fourth table continues the theme of exclusive service to the "lady," and joins it to the notion of honor. This concept of respect for the female is very strong in the writings of Ficino, the Italian Platonist whose work so markedly influenced d'Urfé. It also is one of the principal tenets of the "courtois" ideal, and d'Urfé continues to stress its importance in the next law:

The Fifth Table

Telle soit son affection,
Que même la possession
De ce qu'il désire en son âme,
S'il doit l'acheter au mépris
De son honneur ou de sa dame,
Lui soit moins chère que ce prix.

May his feeling be such,
That even the possession
Of what he desires most in his soul,
If he must secure it in defiance
Of his honor or of his lady,
Would be less dear to him than this prize.

Individual honor, then, is valued along with respect for the woman, and vigilant, rational control is the means to achieve this prize of double esteem, for the mistress and for one's self.

The Sixth Table

Pour sujet qui se vienne offrir,
Qu'il ne puisse jamais souffrir
La honte de la chose aimée:
Et si devant lui par dédain
D'un médisant elle est blamée,
Qu'il meure ou la venge soudain.

Whatever may arise
May he never be able to bear
The shame of his beloved:
And if scornfully in his presence
She is faulted by a slanderer,
May he die or instantly avenge her.

This type of ultimate dictum—death or vengeance, which along with the "bonheur-honneur" motif, seems to anticipate the dilemmas posed by Corneille—reflects both "courtois" and Platonic values, and the degree to which the female's honor must be preserved in the face of social pressure.

The Seventh Table

Que son amour fasse en effet
Qu'il juge en elle tout parfait,
Et quoique sans doute il l'estime
Au prix de ce qu'il aimera,
Qu'il condamne comme d'un crime
Celui qui moins l'estimera.

May his love ensure
That he judges everything to be perfect in her,
And although he, of course, respects her
As measured by his love,
Let him condemn as criminal
He who dares respect her any less.

The seventh table expresses another ideal of the "courtois" code: the lover must believe everything to be perfect in his mistress; and ties to it the idea that the world must also judge her in a highly positive fashion, respecting her as he himself does. The absolute standards of the "code" are maintained, allowing the lover no breach of faith.

The Eighth Table

Qu'épris d'un amour violant,
Il aille sans cesse brûlant,
Et qu'il languisse et qu'il soupire
Entre la vie et le trépas,
Sans toutefois qu'il puisse dire
Ce qu'il veut, ou qu'il ne veut pas.

Smitten by an intense love
Let him burn ceaselessly
And let him languish and sigh
Trapped between life and death,
Without his being able to say
What he wants, or what he doesn't.

The above table reestablishes the Platonic notion of the
life-death struggle in love, positing the link between
the two, yet suggesting also that the lover's psychological state should only border on death. Suicide is not
proposed, for a self-willed death is too extreme and
would cut off the life-love instinct. What is counseled
is a languishing state of self-denial, whereby the life
force is slowly sapped.

The Ninth Table

Méprisant son propre séjour,
Son âme aille vivre d'amour
Au sein de celle qu'il adore,
Et qu'en elle ainsi transformé
Tout ce qu'elle aime et qu'elle honore,
Soit aussi de lui bien aimé.

Scorning his own world,
Let his soul live love
At the breast of his beloved,
And thus transformed into her
All that she cherishes and honors
Should be cherished by him as well.

The union of two into one, the transformation of the lover
into the beloved, these themes are at the heart of Renaissance Platonism. The ninth table demands the total denial of self, in favor of a mystical alliance where the
mistress appears to absorb the former, separate identity

of the lover. Her world alone emerges as sacrosanct; his own is negated.

The Tenth Table

Qu'il tienne les jours pour perdus
Qui loin d'elle sont dépendus.
Toute peine soit embrassée
Pour être en ce lieu désiré,
Et qu'il y soit de la pensée,
Si le corps en est séparé.

Let him consider every day as lost
That is spent away from her.
Let every task be embraced
That allows him to be in the desired place,
And may his mind be there
Even if his body is not.

The tenth table emphasizes spiritual union even when physical presence is not possible. While the latter is considered most desirable (for absence is not perceived here as necessary for the flame to burn), the lover may join his mistress in spirit at all times. True love is thus sustained intact, even if separation occurs.

The Eleventh Table

Que la perte de la raison,
Que les liens et la prison,
Pour elle en son âme il chérisse.
Et se plaise à s'y renfermer
Sans attendre de son service
Que le seul honneur de l'aimer.

May the loss of all reason,
May the chains and prison
For her sake be cherished by him in his soul.
And may he be happy to be bound,
Without anticipating from his service
Anything more than the honor of loving her.

The eleventh table depicts the unreasoning side of love, and thus appears to contradict what Silvandre and Adamas say repeatedly regarding the necessary link between love and reason. This table probably adheres more to "cour-

tois" views, and as such imitates a literary model that
d'Urfé rejected in favor of the Neoplatonic norm. But
his choice of expression here is also metonymical for the
rest of the law, which seeks to establish the totality of
the lover's passive stance.

The Twelfth Table

Qu'il ne puisse jamais penser
Que son amour doive passer:
Qui d'autre sorte le conseille
Soit pour ennemi réputé,
Car c'est de lui prêter l'oreille,
Crime de lèse-majesté.

May he never consider
That his love will end:
Whoever advises him otherwise
Let him be deemed an enemy,
For just listening to him
Is a crime of "lèse-majesté."

[2:181-83]

The final table conveys that love is to be perceived as
boundless; the hyperbole of political crime merely serves
to reinforce the rigorous code to which a true lover must
adhere. His servitude is total.
     The Twelve Tables of the Laws of Love provide in verse
form a summary of the basic precepts guiding a love relationship. Inspired by "courtois" and Renaissance Platonic analysis of love, the laws reflect d'Urfé's effort
to codify love according to their fundamental tenets.
This is the aspect of L'Astrée that has long ensured
its reputation as morally uplifting, as a good reading
selection for young men and particularly young women, and
as a precursor of "préciosité." L'Astrée, however,
is encyclopedic in its exploration of love, and this
philosophically oriented side is only a part of its extensive analysis. Intruding into this vast and wordy domain
is a portrait of love that owes far more to the function
of human desire than is allowed for in the highly
abstract expression of pastoral Platonism. Two things
happen: on the one hand, Silvandre and Adamas's analysis is soundly refuted by Hylas, whose words and actions
point to a radically different conception of love; and,
on the other, the effects of attempting to live by rigid

codes and norms forcefully erupt. Silvandre and Céladon, the "perfect lovers," both fail to achieve the status they had once set out so clearly for themselves. Astrée and Diane also are unable to realize the sublime stature of "la dame." And countless secondary figures are mired in a miserable war between their head and their heart, their mind and their body. The elaborate codes are thus abruptly ruptured.

Chapter Five
Half the Story:
The Narrative Claims

For the reader of the present volume, it is no doubt
apparent by now that there is a relational "gap" between
chapter 2 (on the pastoral influence), chapter 3 (on the
narratives), and chapter 4 (on doctrine). It would be
comforting no doubt to discover that there is a "hidden
harmony" in L'Astrée, to be revealed perhaps in the
remaining sections of the present work. Regrettably,
this is not the case. L'Astrée is a fluctuating,
"unstable" work, a massive enterprise that defies efforts
to synthesize, harmonize, or summarize (1). Thus, many
of the stories related in the third chapter seem only
remotely related, if that, to either the principles of
pastoral fiction or to those of the Neoplatonic love
doctrines so forcefully articulated by Adamas and
Silvandre. In particular, the extreme violence that
erupts in many of the secondary tales, the male aggression that pits itself against female vulnerability, and
the resultant fear of love experienced by many of the
women, appear to contradict the abstract concepts of
spiritual love which are the foundation of Renaissance
Platonic thought. Nor is such seeming contradiction
limited to the aggressive intrusion of violent sexuality
into pastoral Platonism. Equally paradoxical, considering the many words devoted to the ideal of transcendental
union, is the solipsistic anxiety which grips the characters, thrusting heroes and heroines into a world of isolated alienation. The communal world of the pastoral,
the mutual sharing to the extent of self-abnegation,
appear to dissolve in a universe where the self-in-love
seems increasingly depressive and alone.

Honoré d'Urfé makes no effort toward resolving these
apparent paradoxes. There is no "overvoice" which might
lead us to resolution, not even a statement that incon-
sistency is the hallmark of life! Rather, at the point
where an authoritative stance is sought, L'Astrée
falls oddly mute. Admittedly, a search for harmony, a
need to link contradictory parts, is perhaps a modern
phenomenon. Stendhal, for one, would not have struggled

to locate a "center," where there is none! Or perhaps
the division is not between modern and "old world" views,
but rather between alternating epochs whose artistic
perspectives differ broadly. Mme de Lafayette emptied
La Princesse de Clèves of much secondary material, and
produced a concise work which in recent years has enjoyed
great appeal. Classicism is "manageable," at least for
the contemporary reader, whose conditioning is better
suited to concision. The sprawling universes of romantic
fiction deny the reader a single, central focus as they
spin vertiginously out of grasp. So, too, L'Astrée:
encyclopedic, the novel is also inconsistent, irregular,
and parcelized. In d'Urfé's fiction, synthesis is
denied, and perspective is ignored; what emerges is a
total work, whose differing worlds and words coexist,
merge, and then separate, offering a multiple, dizzying
view of the human predicament.

For ultimately, "what happens" in the secondary tales,
and to a large extent in the primary ones as well, has
little to do with pastoral life, with the history of
Forez, with druidism, and most significantly, with the
doctrinal love codes espoused by Adamas and Silvandre,
except insofar as the narratives appear to refute the
functional reality of these codes. Moreover, this seeming "negation" of the Neoplatonic precepts may be only
inferentially assumed, since the author makes no statement to that effect, continuing to allow the doctrinal
level to fill a substantial part of the novel, with no
sense of satire or self-parody ever evident.

D'Urfé intended his novel to be a summa, vast
enough to include metaphysical speculation, local history, exposés on religious customs, and "action" passages
which fly in the face of all the rest. While ignoring
accurate history and metaphysical pronouncements, such
passages remain the very essence of romance, dependent on
sex and violence. It is all there, in what Clifton
Cherpack has called an "often inconsistent compound of
erudition, ideology, and fantasy" (2). D'Urfé was not a
"bad" novelist, unable to focus his material. Rather, he
has denied the concept of a center, in favor of a stunningly baroque structure that is a meeting ground for a
host of Occidental themes and literary forms. In short,
there are several worlds within the book called L'Astrée, worlds of words and worlds of acts, the spiritual
ideal and the libidinal dream, the mind and the body, all
floating in a diffuse vacuum of authorial silence.

It is the intent here to examine in detail much of the
material presented in the two immediate preceding chapters. The narratives, as they are less and less related
structurally to the primary tales, drift away from doctrinal concepts. Gondebaud and Childéric are completely
unconcerned with abstract codes, and lead lives of brutal
aggression and unbridled sexuality, which are censored
only at the very end. Nor is this pattern limited to the
secondary tales; in the primary ones, it is simply less
overt, and far less brutal. For Céladon and Silvandre
are failures in terms of the ideals they have vowed to
cherish. What "happens" to them in their narratives
renders irrelevant the endless words devoted to the formulation of the Neoplatonic and "courtois" doctrines, which
nonetheless, d'Urfé continually holds aloft throughout
his novel, perhaps as a priceless relic, or more likely,
as testimony to man's ability and need to intellectual-
ize, and thereby de-animalize, love.

Thus love, as portrayed in the narratives, is of a
vastly different coloration than in the novel's intellectual jousting. The bulk of the secondary tales focus on
a "trio" situation: most commonly, two men covet one
woman. While the primary tales are not directly dependent on an actualized interruption of Edenic bliss, the
obstacle to happiness is often the fantasized projection
of a trio situation, with both men and women alternately
subjected to "trio" hallucinations.

But the principle of transcendental union is really
denied from the first page of the long novel, where
Honoré d'Urfé quickly sets a tone undermining both
pastoral contentment and Neoplatonic spiritualism. The
exquisite countryside of Forez, with its meandering
rivers, healthy air, fertile land, and rustic charms, is
invaded by the flatterer god, Love, "who quickly changed
his authority into tyranny" [1:9]. This intrusion, which
d'Urfé establishes stylistically as well as thematically, this eruption of the tyrant, is the base for portraying a world gone awry, where Céladon's Twelve Tables of
the Laws of Love have scarcely any functional meaning.
The god alluded to in the Twelve Tables, the sole divinity in a universe consecrated to love, and who, in
Céladon's verse seems a rather benign literary convention, assumes a far more menacing aura elsewhere in L'Astrée, never losing his conventionality perhaps, but
appearing as a force that persistently threatens to
destroy the fragile pastoral world. The tyrant is repeat-

edly depicted as violent and willful, beyond man's control, and utterly manipulative of his behavior.

Such a portrait engenders patterns of behavior which share strikingly little with the "courtois" model. Where the latter postulates a supreme female, whose needs are consistently met by her "chevalier," without his ever violating the sanctity of her person, the narratives offer the vision of characters fearful of, and therefore deformed by, love. Women fear love in L'Astrée, for they perceive that the aggressive sexuality of the males leads to violence and infidelity. The men are apprehensive as well, troubled by the powerful sense of alienation they experience while in love. And both males and females, distrustful of language that is always equivocal or opaque, fear betrayal. Finally, despite Silvandre's wordy assurances that love and jealousy are unrelated, the two coexist superbly well in d'Urfé's book, with all the possibility for mishap inherent to this bond. In such a universe, cast in doubt and self-doubt, distrust, jealousy, and fear, the potential for destruction is enormous. Possible suicide is always at the fringes of L'Astrée, sapping away energies for more positive behavior, if never wholly consummated. In its stead, and fully counter to the transcendental spiritual union posed by Neoplatonism, are solipsistic depression and anxiety so enormous that they often lead either to true insanity or to a state of solitary alienation only one step removed from madness. The world of the narratives is, in short, sexual, violent, jealous, and paranoid—a far cry from the ideals of Silvandre's discourses. We are witnessing the eruption of romance into metaphysics, of one text into another.

The Plight of Women

On the theoretical level, the situation of womankind in L'Astrée meshes harmoniously with the principles of Neoplatonism and "courtoisie." It is awareness of the vulnerable female position that traditionally produces the type of elevated, enlightened thinking associated with both codes. However, women in L'Astrée experience the operative failure of these doctrines to create the secure atmosphere they psychologically and socially require. Their universe is unstable and insecure, providing no sublimated shelter where the word might replace

the act. Even when no gross violation has occurred, the
woman lives in constant anticipation of betrayal and/or
infidelity, recognizing the distressing outcome of male
desire in the lives of her counterparts.
A brief glance at the summaries provided in chapter 3
of the present volume will serve to convey the degraded
situation of L'Astrée's women. Célidée, Cryséide,
Silviane, Daphnide, and Dorinde all experience the reality of violence and unrestrained male sexuality. Often
there is present in the narratives another male figure,
more passive, a friend who wishes to protect her, theo-
retically, from aggressive advances, and who earnestly
attempts to live according to the precepts of Renaissance
love doctrines. But the real story of these women lies
elsewhere: in their determined effort to flee the lust
which Célidée, first, had labeled "monstrous," and which
emanates most frequently from a socially powerful male.
Neoplatonism, like all verbal constructs, by necessity
tends to restrict and tame eroticism, whose atavistic
violence (or potential for that) goes counter to the
ideals of civilized man. Renaissance Platonism may be
seen as one more supreme effort to spiritualize love, to
deny its erotic base, and thus its potential for animal
violence. It has long been a commonplace in d'Urfé
scholarship that his descriptions of physical beauty
remain both conventional and general. Thus, the desirable women are all designated as beautiful, but there is
no description of individualized traits. It is impossible for the reader to conjure up a differentiated image
of Diane or Cryséide or Dorinde. The absence of description, conventional as this choice may be, also seems
designed in d'Urfé's work to filter out any potential
for arousing erotic feelings. The women's—and men's—
nondescriptive beauty would then be a reflection of the
inner radiance they are presumed to possess. To deny
description of face and body is to censor the potential
for arousing less than spiritual emotions. The readers'
inability to fantasize transfers to the characters, who,
we intuitively feel, value this abstract beauty that is
the emblem of inner radiance.
Nonetheless, and despite both thematic and narrative
controls, eroticism, with its connotation of sexual violence, does erupt into the text, and it is the women who
most commonly experience the totality of the aggressive
sexuality left untamed by the Neoplatonic and "courtois"
codes. The result, in the heart of these women, is a

tremendous fear of men and of love which ultimately creates a preference for relationships with other women,
where friendship of the closest nature becomes a sublimated response to fear of heterosexual love. Alternately, women come to seek from their male admirers a
"brotherly" type of affection (such is the case for
Bellinde, Diane's mother), devoid of erotic feelings,
where the "monster" is tamed in favor of a perceived non-
sexual union.

The object of a vicious struggle between Thamire and
Calidon, Célidée disfigures herself to destroy any sexually provocative signs. She becomes an avowed "enemy of
love" [2:61], while aspiring instead to a benign friendship between the sexes. Those who defy the laws of "une
amitié honnête et vertueuse" ("an honest and virtuous
friendship"), she declares, are "burned as if by an
intense fever, and thereby commit scores of crimes"
[2:61]. A victim, too, Cryséide is coveted first by
Clorange, with whom her family has arranged an alliance,
and then by Gondebaud, who throughout L'Astrée assumes
the role of a sexually abusive monarch. Two other royal
princes, Euric and Childéric, also aspire to subjugation
of the female, according to their personal whim. Euric
covets Daphnide, and attempts to seduce her away from his
own faithful knight, Alcidon. And Childéric, the most
contemptible of all, openly desires Silviane, plotting
sexual exploitation of the crudest nature.

While all the males in L'Astrée do not resemble,
overtly in any case, Childéric or Gondebaud, the women
transfer their fear to the whole sex. Thus, Dorinde maintains steadfastly that all men deceive, and she fears
marriage as a subjugation of the self to a despotic
tyrant, who ultimately will not fail to dupe her: "Which
man," she queries rhetorically, "has not deceived the
woman who put her faith in him" [4:62]? Dorinde is the
avowed man-hater of L'Astrée, her resentment trans-
lating an intense fear of betrayal and abandonment. In
her intellectualizing of the problem, she resembles the
characters of Corneille's early plays (traditionally
labeled "comedies"), which recently have been examined
precisely as episodes of fear in the face of passionate
love. Whether or not a common cultural force is involved
may be ascertained only with difficulty, and L'Astrée,
of course, which examines love from multiple perspectives, is a far more comprehensive work than Corneille's
La Place Royale. But one of the major themes, just as

in Corneille, is anxiety over potential betrayal.

Even Phillis, who is perhaps the most suspicion free
character of the novel, and who better than anyone else
psychologically accommodates to infidelity, voices doubt:
"the shepherds of this region dissimulate so well that
too often their heart denies what their mouth promises"
[1:127]. She speaks aphoristically here; and maxim-talk,
with its high investment in linguistic twists, successfully challenges the reality of heartfelt pain by reducing
passion to the level of "saying." The predominance of
intellectual pronouncements on love matters in L'Astrée translates the strong perception of danger to the
self that is at the nucleus of seventeenth-century moral-
istic literature, and not only in the first years of the
century.

For none of the characters is this more evident than
for Astrée and Diane, who, throughout the entire length
of the novel, are able to keep themselves in a state free
of heterosexual entanglements. That they do so, of
course, advances the plot, for union would fail to create
the suspense necessary to romance. But such a delay
could be achieved through devices exterior to the characters' minds. And while, certainly, external obstacles
exist, in the form of parental opposition, these only
serve to reinforce the preexisting mentality of distrust
and fear. Astrée, who seeks the label of "perfect
lover," is one of the most imperious and jealous characters in the book. Her mind is grounded in mistrust, and
despite myriad forms of proof to the contrary, she
remains suspicious of Céladon throughout the novel,
relaxing only in the presence of "Alexis," whom she
believes, or wishes to believe, is female. Nor does she
feign to be any more easygoing than her natural state
suggests. Desire for exclusive possession of the Other
combines with persistent doubt to form a character who
can never be emotionally at peace: "For me, the least
doubt becomes a surety" [1:67], she writes in a self-
analytical letter to Céladon. This missive ultimately
falls into the hands of Galathée, who, ironically, might
be describing her own character as she reads to herself
(and to the book's readers), Astrée's trenchant words!
But even Astrée's doubt is vacillating, never constant
enough to form a personality rebellious toward all loving. Sometimes doubtful, sometimes assured of Céladon's
feelings, as she herself says, Astrée cannot even find
repose in distrust, establishing male betrayal as the

accepted norm and thereby avoiding for herself any emotional entanglement. Rather, her state is an emotionally precarious one, suspended between the two poles of
belief and doubt.

Céladon's efforts to model his behavior after the
"old knights," the knights of the Round Table, who peri-
odically, though fleetingly, are alluded to in d'Urfé's
opus, cannot succeed in a psychological climate where
"service" has meaning only in the most immediate present.
The past, however filled it may be with favors and obli-
gations, is negated by an immediacy that fails to value
the "courtois" model when the least perceived violation
is even rumored. Céladon's suicidal plunge into the
Lignon River is precipitated by Astrée's accusations,
which themselves have no substance and are founded on
mere hearsay. When Sémire betrays, announcing to
Astrée that Céladon is not feigning with Aminthe, but
instead truly desires her, Astrée is all too ready to
believe him, despite many proofs of Céladon's genuine
affection over three years. Indeed, in this universe,
betrayal seems to be expected, anticipated, and thus, on
any hint, is confirmed by minds who need the so-called
reality to sustain the preexistent fear.

Alienation

Fear of betrayal, with the insecurity and anxiety such
a psychological stance implies, is not the only motivat-
ing force in the women's behavior. Or more precisely,
for the female characters fear of betrayal, hatred of
male deception, and anticipation of both, combine with an
awareness of the "lost self" to form a dramatic position
in regard to love matters. This awareness is altered
somewhat for the male, whose alienated state in L'Astrée is more "pure," less tied to fear of lust and of
subsequent abandonment than to a perceived loss of identity. But in both cases, for man and woman alike, there is
real recognition of a type of behavior that he or she
believes is inconsistent with a "former" level of the
self. Thus, while Diane may be every bit as vehement as
Dorinde in her account of male sexuality and inconstancy
[4:70-71], she joins to this bitterness and surveillance
of her own behavior, a sharp awareness of how "different"
she is in and out of love. Attuned to the demands of
passionate love when she herself was emotionally indiffer-

ent, Diane—whose very name is emblematic of the cold,
refusing female—recognizes that her feelings for
Silvandre have led her to a state of being previously
unknown to her. She has fallen victim to a nonrational
state of mind, where the constraints she once had imposed
on herself are no longer viable. Previously aware and
fearful of men's flattery, careful to avoid losing herself to unfaithful men, now that she has fallen in love
with Silvandre she can only attempt to depict, inexplica-
bly, her fall from grace. Convinced that she has in fact
been betrayed by Silvandre (on a false rumor spread by
Laonice), Diane sees herself upset to the point of irra-
tionality: "Oh Diane . . . when I observe you closely, I
no longer recognize you, finding nothing in you of that
earlier Diane you once were, except the name Diane . . .
if I am no longer Diane, who have I then become? The
opposite . . . of the Diane I used to be" [4:47-48]. Her
sense of alienation, which she correctly perceives as a
negation of a former, tranquil state, lost now to fren-
zied jealousy and imagined woes, is the result of a
specifically female context: that is, perceived loss of
self for women is tied to an awareness of their vulnerability. The very potential for abandonment creates in
these women anxious fantasies of betrayal. But it is not
only being discarded that is feared. Rather, such anxiety may create a more fundamental awareness that transcends sexual distinction, and to which the shepherds of
L'Astrée, with the exception of Hylas, are prone.
      Silvandre, Diane's partner in love and ostensibly the
most intellectual of the male protagonists, parallels his
mistress in an awareness of a lost state of (human)
grace. His reactions to rumors of Diane's infidelity—
false rumors again—reflect his perception of how much
emotional liberty he has lost. Physically distressed,
he is suddenly prone to fainting spells, a corporal
reaction which translates his out-of-self-control state
of being. His lucidity is still sufficient for him
to recognize the limits of reason in a world gone haywire from too much loving. No longer the "absolute
master of his thought process" [2:8], and no longer in
sole control of his life, Silvandre is nonetheless able
to state clearly his substantial loss. Other male characters in L'Astrée cannot, so lost are they to the
world and to themselves that lucidity becomes an irrelevant quality for their existence. Called back to reason
by friends and counselors, such male figures nonetheless

persist in choosing alienation over self-understanding.
Céladon's Twelve Tables, which codify Neoplatonic and
"courtois" doctrines, may be viewed as the poetic, conventional expression of spiritualized love. Reading through
them, one does not focus on their separate or individual
literality; rather, the Tables together form a written
portrait of idealized, abstract love. The overall meaning of the Tables is that of Love's totality, and of the
true Lover's posture of submission to his mistress.
Allusions in the Tables to alienation, madness, and death
seem to function only rhetorically, conventionally, and
even metonymically, as components in a composite picture
of absolute fidelity and servitude. The lover's complete
involvement is the idea conveyed by the Tables, and the
reader (or auditor) focuses less on any one individual
prescription than on the overall image of eternal love
and self-denial. In short, the Twelve Tables appear as
yet one more example of a long-standing, Occidental
textual tradition: the formulation and sanctioning of
spiritualized, sublimated love.

When, however, the male characters of Astrée act,
when they move beyond the level of the word, their comportment is inevitably a literal, not rhetorical, reflection of the Laws of Love. Instead of a picture of
sublime fidelity and submission, their lives convey only
decomposition and disintegration, leading toward ultimate
death. While suicide per se is evaded in L'Astrée,
death cravings and suicide substitutes form an integral
part of the text. Indeed, L'Astrée opens on such a
note: Céladon's plunge into the Lignon is a sign of the
death wish which hangs over the whole novel. Excessive
and conventional in a literary sense, such a gesture nonetheless conveys the despair and self-destruction which,
in L'Astrée, are never wholly absent.

Thus, allusion to death, as in the Twelve Tables, is
no longer metonymic. Céladon's suicidal plunge establishes early on in the work the results of a literal
reading of the love codes. Death is no longer merely
emblematic of the lover's desired self-abnegation. It is
instead a force which continually holds great fascination
for the lovers, and as such dissipates their vital energy. Hence, often flirtation with suicide occurs in a
slow, drawn-out fashion, resulting in both physical and
psychological disintegration. Céladon's jump into the
Lignon is at once too dramatic and too limited for com-
municating the slow breaking apart of the self. D'Urfé

prefers to dwell on Céladon's life after he has been
rescued from drowning by Galathée, and after he has successfully escaped from her palace. It is at this point
that Céladon becomes a virtual hermit, wandering aimlessly in the forest, scarcely eating, lost to the world and
to himself. Nor is this the first time he seeks isolation and deprivation. Shortly after the first voyeuristic episode, when, disguised as a girl, he is able to
judge Astrée in a beauty contest, Céladon is rebuffed
by the young woman. At the first sign of rejection, he
retires to the woods, for it is only there that he may
find a balm for his pain. It takes surprisingly little
for the male characters to sink into deep depression.
Their poor psychological state is frequently the result
of unfounded, but extreme jealousy, and of their failure
to clarify. Thus, Lycidas, believing that Silvandre
covets Phillis as he himself does, retreats to the woods,
"alone, to meditate on his sad thoughts" [2:25]. For
both Céladon and Lycidas, depression is engendered by a
loss of will, which continues to feed the distorted mind,
thereby sustaining a morbid view of self and world. The
result is a continuing paralysis which prohibits the male
from acting to discover the truth, a state of blindness
that he paradoxically seems to crave.
     The reasons for such behavior are complex. Essential-
ly, the male protagonists are passive figures, whose
indecision and inability to act reflect the apparent
dominance of the female. Both Jean Charron and Jacques
Ehrmann have accurately depicted this state of affairs,
whereby the men flounder and the women control. Ehrmann,
particularly, stresses the close relationship between the
Renaissance Platonic and "courtois" codes and the failure
of the male to assert himself: "In L'Astrée, woman
worship depends wholly on the male renouncing his virility" (3). Thus, Céladon, in a lengthy monologue, wonders
why he cannot disavow the Alexis mask and move toward an
open declaration to Astrée. The analysis of his choice
is lucid, reflecting his own withered masculinity: "if
there is something that keeps you happy, isn't it knowing
in your soul that never have you failed to observe the
laws of perfect love" [3:605-6]? The code of loving,
then, as posited in Céladon's Twelve Tables, and elaborated throughout L'Astrée by Adamas and Silvandre, becomes the surpreme arbiter, negating behavioral patterns
perceived as deviant. But this occurs at a cost, for
Céladon's desire to adhere is also an obstacle to trans-

parence, to genuine communication transcending the opaque screen which lies over the whole novel. Of course, were he to strive for such communication with Astrée, the work as we know it could not proceed, for L'Astrée is built on a wobbly foundation of distrust and deception. Nonetheless, d'Urfé chooses a willed sublimation—adherence to the code rather than an effort at consummation of the relationship—to create the obstacle necessary to avoid closure. As such, one can only suspect that Céladon, too, is governed by a fear of love so powerful that he creates actively his own impediments, where even no outer ones exist. Thus, Adamas's efforts at persuading the young shepherd to disavow his sham, to renounce "Alexis" for Céladon, come to naught, for Céladon appears to covet, subconsciously perhaps, the disguise that allows for a literal adherence to the code and therefore for an intriguing emotional distance, where voyeurism and not commitment is the desired goal. The code becomes an escape, reflecting a fear of genuine loving and of acting, at least beyond the level of travesty.

At other moments in L'Astrée, male passivity may be seen as more closely aligned with a death wish than with role playing. Céladon's plunge into the Lignon is one such example, as is his morbid, solitary wandering. Secondary characters, too, reflect this tendency toward introspection and isolation which ultimately serve to block both life and love. Hence, Damon wanders aimlessly throughout Europe and Africa, sure that Madonte has betrayed him; and he would doubtless die of lassitude and depression were he not repeatedly called back to life by his manservant. The solitary, moribund self may also die for the world while remaining physically alive. Céladon skirts madness, his life in the woods reflecting a willed alienation; but figures such as Adraste and Rosiléon go completely mad from love, their insanity a grave testimony to the self-abnegation written in the Twelve Tables. The form of loving that these characters adopt, or which is meted out to them by a vague Fate, denies self-preservation in favor of a perceived purity of intention. But for the reader, the impression is one of male retreat to a dangerous psychological level. Self-hatred, resulting in extreme self-abnegation, appears to lead to a slow sapping of the life force. And since, in so many instances, such extreme lack of self-preservation is founded on spurious hearsay, one can only suspect that death is as equally attractive a force as love. The

literal interpretation of the code leads, then, to a
withered, passive male, unable or unwilling to assume a
stance leading to clarification, communion, and consummation.

The Social Climate: Parents, Spies, and Voyeurs

The failure to realize communication, and thereby
mutual love, may be explained by external, socially
imposed constraints as well as by psychological ones born
of the individual. While the former would be impotent to
dictate behavioral patterns were it not for the pervasive
fear and distrust generated by the self, the constraints
and obstacles imposed from "outside"—that is, from the
social unit—intensify the more menacing, if less tangible, psychological anxieties. Ultimately, this social
impediment merges with the inherent fear of abandonment,
and of love itself, to create a general schema of nonconsummation and hence, of the erotic suspense necessary to
this novel and to all romance.

In L'Astrée, the primary source of external obstacles is the family unit. Parental opposition to the
designs of the young couple is rampant, often assuming
threatening and even sadistic forms. The cruel mother of
Cryséide makes repeated efforts to assure her daughter's
marriage to Clorange, who is wealthy, but physically
repelling for his deformities. And Silvanire's obsessive
father, insistent that his daughter wed rich Théante,
allows her to marry Aglante, whom she loves, only when
the girl falls deathly ill. His machinations are endless, however, for when she recovers, he attempts to
annul that marriage in order to ensure the match with
Théante. Parental opposition in L'Astrée is most
often based on values pertaining to money and class (in
clear opposition to the classless society portrayed in
traditional pastoral literature). One parent wishes the
child to marry for great wealth, although the cruelty of
this intention captures a more subconscious hatred for
the offspring, which the fairy tale (a favorite genre in
seventeenth-century France) so eloquently portrayed.
Another—and this is the case for Bellinde, Diane's
mother—refuses to sanction a marriage when birth, class
status, and wealth are in doubt. "So as to preserve the
purity of each class unit, certain marriages will be
denied," writes Jacques Ehrmann (4). For him, these

class determined decisions form the sole invariable in an
otherwise free-floating universe. I questioned earlier
this view of a "baroque" world, but it is not necessary
to conclude as Ehrmann does to detect the vital importance of class to the characters, at least to parents—
and sometimes to the children as well. Diane, for one,
continues to espouse her mother's opinions throughout
much of the novel, and rejects Silvandre on the basis of
his unknown past and hazy present.

Parental intransigence is thus a major external impediment to the union of the couple. In the secondary narratives—those of Silvanire and Cryséide, for example—
it is sufficient to remove the obstacle posed by the
parent for the couple to maintain union. Once a judgment
has been rendered against Silvanire's father, stipulating
that he cannot use his power tyranically, Aglante and
Silvanire are free. In the primary narratives, however,
parental opposition is not, in and of itself, sufficient
to create a block. Here, it joins with internal distress
to form a complex halt to union. Even when Diane is
freed from the obsessive concern of adhering faithfully
to her mother's wishes, her relationship with Silvandre
flounders in a psychological climate of distrust, fear,
and jealousy. Nonetheless, even in the principal tales,
the family serves to impede union, and its voyeuristic
impulses are all too often interiorized by the victims
themselves.

Indeed, there are voyeurs and spies all through L'Astrée. The so-called idyllic world is penetrated by
lookers and listeners whose role it is to deny all that
is secret and intimate, in favor of public revelation.
It becomes impossible to conceal, for society imposes
itself everywhere, denying a retreat to the individual
and the couple. Among the best spies are parents, particularly Alcippe, who, determined to block Céladon's relationship with Astrée, manages to be everywhere they are.
He locates their secret hiding places; he finds and
reads their private letters. Alcippe's spying is all the
more troublesome in that greed—so conventional a force—
does not motivate him. Rather, his opposition stems from
the personal grudge he holds against Alcé, Astrée's
dead father, for their own dispute of long ago. Out of
vengeful pride, and jealousy perhaps, he is ready to
sacrifice the young couple's happiness, joining in his
feelings the myriad parents of myth and fairy tale eager
to block their children's fulfillment.

Like Diane, moreover, the children who are the victims
of these machinations are remarkably subservient. To
fool Alcippe, Astrée and Céladon invent only games,
which in most cases are readily discovered by the father.
This is the extent of their rebellion. Only in part 4
is there an overt revolt against authoritative stances,
but this rebellion is displaced onto secondary figures.
Godomar pits himself directly against his father
Gondebaud, whom the son sees as a threat to his own
future. And Rosiléon refuses to wed Céphise, although
King Policandre has ordered the match. Elsewhere, intransigence holds sway, while the children vacillate.

Nor is parental intervention the sole means to deny
Edenic bliss. The whole social network seemingly has an
investment in uncovering and discovering the most private
confidences. And, paradoxically, the very person who
seeks to guard the sanctitiy of a love secret, may be
found observing and even publicizing the secret of
another. Of course, L'Astrée is wholly dependent on a
closed communications network to advance its plots and
subplots. Narrative omniscience (apparent elsewhere in
the novel) is in these instances replaced by polyphonism,
with each character observing and then publicizing events
to which he or she is a party as a "see all—hear all"
narrator, not as a participant, except when that character in turn becomes a performer, observed by someone
else. In this universe, privacy is impossible, lost in
the communal society which forms the base of the pastoral
world. The complete inability to preserve a "space" of
one's own is reflected in this curious passage from the
second part, where d'Urfé, in an effort either at self-
parody or at conveying the infernal presence of Everyone
(or perhaps wishing to achieve both), presents a seemingly endless list of "voyeurs" and "écouteurs," each alternately spy and victim:

> Thus, walking down toward the plain we caught sight of
> Silvandre who, seated by some trees, was so absorbed
> in singing and in playing his pipes, that he was un-
> aware of Diane, who, recognizing his voice, had
> slipped behind the thicket to listen, but without
> being observed. And Diane was so eager to hear him
> that she didn't see Astrée and Phillis who were watch-
> ing her maneuvers, and who, reacting to an identical
> whim, moved to another side, so as not to be detected
> by either Diane or Silvandre. And we observed with

great pleasure Lycidas, who, perched on slightly higher ground, was watching Phillis creep slowly along, so
as not to be seen by Silvandre. [2:299]

In this tableau of spying, described and therefore published by Léonide, who is part of the "we" of the final
sentence, each self is prey to another who insists on
surprising and thereby violating secret thoughts and
acts. Conveyed through pantomime, this portrait of the
ever-present and intrusive Other serves to communicate
the very public nature of all love matters in L'Astrée.
    Spies, in fact, not only observe voyeuristically:
they are also avid letter readers. Discretion is totally
impossible when lovers attempt to put their feelings into
words. By its very nature, a letter is an ambiguous
form: intended as a private, intimate expression, a
missive may at any moment fall into another's hands,
thereby revealing its contents and becoming public. In
L'Astrée, which advances plot by means of correspondence, letters almost always become public, and are usually "published" verbatim in the larger text. The reader,
too, becomes an interloper, penetrating a private world,
or at least the illusion of one, since obviously the
reader of the novel is an invited guest! In fact, the
entire narrative of Astrée and Céladon is based on the
interruption and publication of their intimate letters.
Alcippe finds and reads the letters; Léonide steals them
and "publishes" their contents; Sémire discovers a letter from Astrée to Céladon, and constructs his entire
betrayal on this find. Letters in L'Astrée are inevitably stolen, read, copied (thus committing them to public display forever), and may even be forged, an act
which totally negates the premise of genuine and private
communication.
    There are listeners, seers, readers, and forgers
throughout L'Astrée, all a threat to the sanctity of
individual and couple. This is a highly restrained
locus, the sense of enclosure is paramount, and yet, to
escape (that is, to leave the boundaries of Forez), is to
leave the narrative. Indeed, the basic movement of the
novel is in the opposite direction: toward Forez, for it
is only here that resolution may occur. But Forez the
paradise becomes Forez the hell, censuring and subverting
the very love it is supposed to protect. In itself such
spying is sufficiently troubling, leading to massive

insecurity among the book's diverse characters. Yet more
disquieting, however, is that the spying, which is initiated from outside, that is, from the family or larger
social unit, may become interiorized, with the result
that the victim of spying begins to observe his or her
own predicament! Ehrmann touches on this when he writes
that "the most profound sense of illusion (such is the
case of Astrée) results from the characters becoming
spectators of their own spectacle. Their subjugation is
then complete" (5). Ehrmann's statement, however, maintains the "outer" perspective of a spectacle, rather than
conveying the "inner" subversion which is at its root.
For it is here that the two threats—one socially imposed, the other individually generated—merge completely. Astrée, on the advice of treacherous Sémire, does
in effect become a "spy," treating herself to the spectacle of Céladon with Aminthe. But this experience occurs
only because Astrée has already interiorized the atmosphere of distrust and doubt which permeates the novel.
Her reasons for spying on the very scene she herself
created—for it was Astrée, after all, who first formulated the Céladon-Aminthe fiction—are based not on any
social opposition, but rather on the suspicious state
that is the very foundation of L'Astrée. Her watchful-
ness, which imitates perfectly that of Alcippe, is the
externalized experience of distrust, jealousy, and fear.
Spying in L'Astrée usually connotes an outside, socially imposed censure; but for Astrée, the act now assumes
a psychological dimension which reflects only her own
distraught state: the "outer" and "inner" manifestations
of suspicion are hereby joined.

Hylas's Role

Is there, then, in L'Astrée, no foil, no adroitly
conceived "corrective" to this otherwise pervasive atmosphere of joyless loving? There is—in the person of
Hylas—an extension of yet another Occidental literary
tradition: the unfaithful, but happy lover, the free
spirit. Despite this ostentatious portrait of infidelity, however, d'Urfé persistently leaves his character
uncensured and even uncriticized. (Only Baro, clearly
squeamish about his predecessor's silences, chooses to
correct Hylas, who in the novel's fifth part is presented
as "wayward.") In d'Urfé's four parts, Hylas's views

are consistently presented at regular intervals; he is a
practiced theoretician, like Silvandre, and an excellent
debator. His philosophy, moreover, finds operational
space in his life, unlike the abstract speculations of
Silvandre, who, as Hylas correctly perceives, fails to
rely on experience as master. But this functional success does not imply that d'Urfé is supportive of Hylas's
views, to the exclusion of all others. Here, as elsewhere, Honoré d'Urfé maintains an authorial vacuum,
only presenting, never condemning or praising. Hylas
should not therefore be seen in contrapuntal fashion to
Silvandre-Céladon. He is really not a corrective to the
code of absolute fidelity, but rather an alternative.
Hylas is simply "other." As the essence of infidelity,
he incarnates other values, other systems, and thereby
reflects other textual traditions.

That Hylas enjoys a privileged place in L'Astrée is
clear throughout d'Urfé's four parts. He "possesses"
his own narrative, and his tale also interrupts and inter-
twines with a large number of primary and secondary narratives. He is everywhere in the text. Indeed, Hylas's
major distinguishing trait is that he has loved everywhere. All are familiar with his vast reputation, if
they have not experienced firsthand his amorous techniques. He has, in short, dispersed his seed through all
of southern France, seducing and abandoning with remarkable ease. Along the way, he has developed a curious
theory of loving, one that in its "bourgeois" predilection clearly challenges the idealism of the aristocratic
Renaissance Platonic code. Comparing his love to money,
Hylas seeks to dispense each according to the value of
the desired object:

When I undertake to love a woman, I verify her beauty,
for, as you know, the worth of women is in beauty
alone. And immediately, I make a pile of love in my
soul, equal to her value and worth, and when in love,
I spend this pile. At the point I have used all that
I saved for her, no more remains for that woman. If I
wish to love again, I must seek out another beauty to
form another pile of love, so, in this matter, my
money and my love are very much alike. I mean that
for both, once they are spent, I possess them no more.
. . . [3:348]

Hylas's seminal dispersion, couched in this imagery

which both conceals and reveals its sexual origin, is at
odds with the rigid constancy preached over and over
again in L'Astrée. Yet his voice is hardly an unfamiliar one. Western literature is filled with echoes of
this theme. Jean Rousset has convincingly linked the
portrait of Hylas, as composed by d'Urfé, to the early
seventeenth-century, European-wide fascination with movement, flux, and transformation. The poetry of John
Donne, Du Perron, Lubrano, Gongora, and Marino all
reflect this cultural obsession with Protean forms.
Rousset also ties Hylas to the figure of Don Juan,
although he adds that d'Urfé's character lacks the
religious and mythical dimensions of the seducer par
excellence. Rousset's intention is to place Hylas
within a cultural and literary framework, and also to
establish Hylas's enormous appeal in early seventeenth-
century France (6). But Hylas may be linked not only to
the "baroque" thematics of shift and flux, but additionally to a related tradition that stresses the value of
inconstancy, in a moral sense. Hylas's relativistic,
less demanding views, his readiness to love anywhere and
everywhere, and the psychological liberation of such a
stance, reflect a pleasure-oriented tradition, deep in
Western thought, that elevates the joyful life and posits
an existence free of the constraints of conventional
morality, authority, and social censure. At the base of
his thinking lies a firm opposition to the concept of
absolute fidelity in love, and, concomitantly, to the
concept of possession. Pitilessly attacking what he
perceives to be enervating and even destructive principles, Hylas creates in L'Astrée a mini-world, no
larger than himself and Stelle, whereby the values of
Neoplatonic and "courtois" thought are turned on their
head, and whereby even the language of those abstract,
absolute codes is readily negated. A word change here or
there, as his parody of the Twelve Tables shows, is sufficient to counter the trend toward solipsism, depression,
and morbidity. Hylas, of course, converts no one, just
as he remains true to his own principles forever, indifferent to the moralism of Silvandre or Adamas. His ideas
are isolated in the text, yet taken together they form
one more exclusive system in the occidental tradition,
wholly separate and distinct from Silvandre's precepts.
There is, moreover, no meeting ground for these radically
dissimilar discourses.

Hylas's Tale

Similar to many of the major characters in L'Astrée, Hylas has a history. Unlike them, however, he also has a "past." The latter is in part explained by the former, which assumes the form of parental conditioning. Parents are a permanently troubling element in L'Astrée, for not only do they oppose love matches, they also condition their offspring, marking them permanently (or at least until the book's end). If Silvandre's unstable, social identity is the result of his not knowing who his parents are, so, too, Hylas extends into adulthood, or late adolescence, certain traits associated with his mother. In L'Astrée, little attention is given over to child-hood, yet odd bits of significant patterns may be glimpsed. Hylas was raised as the spoiled only child of a mother who worshipped him. The male-centered universe created by her becomes the sole emotional reality for the boy, who, from an early age (as he himself allows), imagines that all women are his. Hylas's own narrative, in which he describes his past amorous adventures, is filled with a seemingly endless list of female names, the multiciplicity of women suggesting only their sheer inter-changeability. His "philosophy," as such, begins to be articulated and intellectualized in reference to these patterns begun in early youth.

It is not feasible to read Hylas's tale without a sense of dismay at all those female names! Moreover, he dupes and betrays most of the women—only occasionally does the reverse occur. No great harm is done, it is true, for the women seem to survive rather well, and some, such as Dorinde, even come to view him as the least hypocritical male she has ever encountered. Nonetheless, his opinions and actions may be particularly odious to modern sensibilities, as perhaps they were also to the "précieuses," who admired best those sections of L'As-trée which censored infidelity, male lust, and deceit. As a classic seducer, Hylas inevitably lends himself to overt criticism of his mores. And his pleasure-oriented character, which he never dissimulates, and indeed which is often presented in off-color terms, will always offend those of a more "puritanical," or even classically liber-al, bent.

Nevertheless, a "moral" reading of Hylas's role in the

novel would fail to establish the totality of what he
represents. While his abusive side is always apparent,
there is another factor which tempers Hylas's infideli-
ties. No Don Juan, whose deceit and treachery assume far
more menacing tones, Hylas loves and leaves while stipulating the integral liberty of both partners. Witness
his unique interpretation of the unhappy adventures of
Cryséide and Arimant, whose happiness was menaced by the
lecherous Gondebaud: "And would it not have been better,
without each causing the other so much suffering, for
Cryséide to have become queen of the Burgundians
[through a marriage to Gondebaud], since once she possessed Gondebaud's heart, she would eventually and
prudently have been able to give to her Arimant all the
satisfaction he could have desired" [3:469]? Such an
easy, practical solution, and frankly an appealing one,
too, after a drawn-out narrative of some hundred pages,
which leaves both characters and readers drained!
Hylas's option, in the context where it appears, is subversive, a clear threat to the value of ultimate sexual
fidelity. At the same time, however, he correctly labels
the emotional waste which results from a too literal
interpretation of the codes. As Hylas continues to
speak, he proclaims Silvandre's fundamental error in his
analysis of Cryséide's predicament: "Do you really
know, Silvandre, where all their unhappiness and trouble
originated? In the nonsense that you label fidelity:
that alone tormented them for so many years . . ." [3:
469-70].

Hylas's attack on fidelity does not stem from abstract
criticism of traditional moral norms. Rather, if he continues to voice his theory of infidelity throughout the
four long volumes, it is because he categorically rejects
the depressive anxiety of lovers who commit themselves to
the Platonic and "courtois" ideals. Scorning the introspection and morbidity which inevitably follow an effort
to live by such idealism, Hylas posits the joys of a
pleasure oriented life and thereby establishes the primary value as self-preservation. In yet another "joust"
with his favorite opponent, Silvandre, Hylas queries
rhetorically: "For why does one bother to love if not
for the sake of happiness? And what pleasure can these
sad and pensive lovers know, all emotionally strung out,
their mind and heart consumed with this chimera of infidelity? . . . Oh, my friends, tell me, what wild beast
is this infidelity? whom has it ever devoured?" [2:384].

For Hylas, infidelity is nothing more than a figment of
the imagination, a consuming fear suffered by those who
lack experience in love matters.

There are several corollaries to Hylas's basic theo-
rem. Most significant is the value he places on "mediocre" loving, by which he means a less intense experience
than that sought by the novel's other lovers. The perfect bliss held out by the Renaissance Platonists as the
absolute ideal of love, is rejected in favor of a more
relative position counseling moderation and self-control
as the means to true pleasure. It is clear that this
effort to avoid highly intense forms of love is subversive in its violation of the Edenic myth as it exists
throughout d'Urfé's work. Yet, rather than appearing as
negative or destructive, Hylas's views emerge as only
"sensibly subversive." His words blow a breath of air,
of life, into an otherwise closed and suffocating universe, split between endless abstractions and erotic
fantasies which are either violently destructive (as for
Gondebaud and Childéric), or frustrating in the extreme
(as for Céladon disguised as Alexis). "Mediocre" loving
thus reveals itself as ultimately life-sustaining, and,
paradoxically perhaps, fulfilling, for it denies the
essential concept of possession, forever unattainable
given the fundamental liberty of each individual. To
love as Hylas does is to acknowledge that very liberty:
in union, each partner maintains a healthy independence.

Perhaps equally significant is Hylas's acceptance of a
lost love, as he analyzes not only his own fickleness,
but that of his partners as well: "the loss of or change
in a relationship has scarcely ever caused me to despair,
since I have always maintained a certain resolve and courage which didn't allow me to wallow in sadness for such
an accident" [3:351-52]. His use of the word "courage"
here may seem oddly misplaced, but he uses it frequently
to describe his own state of mind as opposed to the flab-
by retreats of Céladon and Silvandre. The desire for
absolute fidelity to the Code, which these two characters
strive to realize, leads to a withered, passive male, who
finds his sole means to action in a curious transvestism.
Alternately, such male figures are fainters or seekers
of death. When Hylas claims that he "alone knows how to
love as a spirited and courageous man" [2:385], he appears to be depicting a life force so strong that it must
reject the dissipating, enervating love which Silvandre
experiences with Diane. Hylas constructs a vigorous

virility against the claims of denial and death, and in
so doing creates not only the reign of fickleness—that
would be too superficially limiting—but of life itself.
Finally, just as the love experience itself is founded
on a relativism which denies the rigorous standards of
the Code, so, too, in this context is beauty conceived as
a nonabsolute state. The concept of beauty in L'Astrée is complex, bound as it is to the larger value systems which encompass it. Thus, the abstract and visually
unimaginable (for the reader) beauty which permeates the
Platonic and "courtois" modes, reflects the cerebral love
counseled by Adamas and Silvandre. Beauty is not only an
abstraction in their words, it is the product solely of
language constructs based on superlatives (all variants
of "the most beautiful . . ."). There is never a tangible feel to this beauty, or Beauty, for to endow it
materially would be to deny its status as Idea, thereby
evoking a potential sexual link. For Hylas, however,
there is no Beauty, only beauty, and it is defined solely
in reference to himself. What moves him is, by defini-
tion, beautiful: "I only label beauty that which
pleases, and if Stelle alone pleases me more than all
other women . . . isn't it true that she possesses more
beauty for me . . ." [4:707]? The final two words of
this statement highlight the principal source of all
judgments in Hylas's emotional universe: the self.
Detached from the abstractly aesthetic world of Renaissance Platonism, beauty becomes a certain woman, a particular woman, who is capable of engendering pleasure in a
particular male. No longer the Idea, or even an idea, it
is now a sexually based principle, individual and potentially even idiosyncratic.

Hylas's Love Laws

THE TWELVE CONDITIONS OF LOVE. The codified formulation of Hylas's opinions occurs twice. In the third part
of L'Astrée, Hylas, now in love with Stelle, postulates "The Twelve Conditions by which Stelle and Hylas
promise to love each other henceforth." Based on the
conviction that most lovers' "anger and quarrels come
from the tyranny which each partner seeks to maintain
over the other" [3:490], the Twelve Conditions challenge
forcefully the tenets of the Neoplatonic code. Together,
they stipulate each individual's inherent liberty:

Neither partner will usurp sovereign authority over the other, which we say is tyranny.

Each of us will be simultaneously the beloved and the lover, the lover and the beloved.

Our friendship will be forever free of constraint.

We shall love each other for as long as we so feel.

The one who wishes to quit loving may do so, without blame for infidelity.

When we wish, without destroying our relationship, we may love whomever we choose, and, for as long as we wish, we may continue this relationship or freely abandon it.

All jealousy, complaints, and sadness will be banished between us, as incompatible with our perfect friendship.

When conversing we shall be free, and each of us will do and say as we so desire, free of constraint, without troubling the other.

In order to be neither liars nor slaves, in act or in word, all expressions such as "fidelity," "servitude," and "eternal affection," will never appear in our speech.

Both of us, or one of us, may continue or not continue to love.

If this relationship breaks off, on one side or on both, we may renew it when we please.

In order to be spared long-standing love or hatred, we shall be obliged to forget both services and disservices. [3:490-91]

The form of loving conceived by Hylas and Stelle, valuing freedom rather than eternal fidelity, has, of course, enjoyed a long life in Western thought. "Free love" partisans continue to challenge the liberal tradition of monogamy. The antagonism between the two groups remains

substantial to this day. In L'Astrée, Silvandre is
driven almost to frenzy by Hylas's Twelve Conditions,
claiming that he does not even wish to hear them. Yet,
he understands only too well their subversive nature when
contrasted with his own values; and it is he who formulates the ultimate condition of freedom, in a statement
so totally nihilistic that it destroys the very foundation of Hylas's thinking, leaving in its stead a complete
vacuum: "Nonetheless, we, Stelle and Hylas, are so careful to preserve our freedom, and are such ardent enemies
of constraint, that we shall be permitted, when we so
choose, to observe not a single one of the above described conditions" [3:494]! Here, the Twelve Conditions,
themselves too rigid for a code stipulating total freedom, receive their ultimate corollary, which severs their
link to any form of obligation.
    The implication of Hylas's views is never entirely
clear. Contemporary thought has exposed the potential
for psychological damage that exists when individual freedom becomes the highest value. One lover may indeed wish
to "bind" exclusively, while the other chooses a multiplicity of partners. Hylas's system is highly narcissistic,
allowing no room for pain, if one partner but not the
other chooses "free love." Typically, however, d'Urfé
offers no further explanation or judgment, writing only
that Hylas and Stelle did enjoy a happy relationship,
born in and carried out in freedom [3:494]. This is the
only hint—and it is no more than that—of a more viable
alternative to love than that described by the novel's
intellectuals. Nonetheless, little should be made of
this sketchy allusion to the couple's happiness, for, as
stated earlier, Hylas and Stelle's system continues to
function in virtual isolation, convincing no one, at best
frequently amusing to the audience and spectators, sometimes repelling to them. Between the discourse of Hylas,
and that of Silvandre—each the essential reflection of
yet other texts and other words—there is only a very
large gap.
    THE TWELVE TABLES OF THE LAWS OF LOVE, AC-
CORDING TO HYLAS. Throughout d'Urfé's four long parts,
Hylas repeats his basic premise associating love with
freedom. But he also returns frequently to discussing
the sheer ease of loving. Where, for Céladon, Astrée,
Lycidas, Diane, and Silvandre, love is an arduous, difficult proposition, for Hylas nothing is more facile, since

nothing is more natural. The proliferation of female names throughout Hylas's own narrative contrasts with the compulsive sameness and repetition of the Céladon-Astrée story. The ease with which Hylas confronts and endures the experience of love is codified, both thematically and structurally, in his Twelve Tables, where he alters the wording and thereby the premises of Céladon's testimony to eternally faithful love.

Such word manipulation is rare in L'Astrée. Once language is written it generally is indelible in this text. Letters are kept, they circulate, they are often read aloud by others than the intended recipient, frequently damning the sender. Names are carved into tree trunks, never to be erased, a permanent sign of absolute and eternal love. Nonetheless, with Hylas's Twelve Tables, altering of language does occur, as Hylas shifts or changes a word here or there! But the transformed phrase does not imply only a slight alteration of meaning, despite the ease with which Hylas proceeds. Rather, what emerges from his tinkering is a radical denial of the absolute values posited earlier by Céladon.

Included here are three examples of Hylas's laws, which, for the sake of comparison, are preceded by the corresponding laws of Céladon. (The English translation of Hylas's laws appears in the notes.) They are particularly good examples of how minor structural shifts will create a dramatic negation of original meaning:

Third Table

Céladon
Bornant en lui tous ses plaisirs,
Qu'il arrête tous ses désirs
Au service de cette belle,
Voire qu'il cesse de s'aimer,
Sinon que d'autant qu'aimé d'elle,
Il se doit pour elle estimer.

Hylas
Ne bornant jamais ses désirs,
Qu'il cherche partout des plaisirs,
Faisant toujours amour nouvelle,
Voire qu'il cesse de l'aimer
Sinon que d'autant qu'aimé d'elle,
Pour lui seul il doit l'estimer.

Eighth Table

Céladon
Qu'épris d'un amour violent
Il aille sans cesse brûlant,
Et qu'il languisse et qu'il soupire
Entre la vie et le trépas,
Sans toutefois qu'il puisse dire
Ce qu'il veut, ou qu'il ne veut pas.

Hylas
Qu'épris d'un amour assez lent,
In n'aille sans cesse brûlant,
Ni qu'il languisse ou qu'il soupire
Entre la vie at le trépas:
Mais que toujours il puisse dire
Ce qu'il veut, ou qu'il ne veut pas.

Twelfth Table

Céladon
Qu'il ne puisse jamais penser
Que son amour doive passer:
Qui d'autre sorte le conseille
Soit pour ennemi réputé,
Car c'est de lui prêter l'oreille,
Crime de lèse-majesté.

Hylas
Qu'il ne puisse jamais penser
Que tel amour n'ait à passer:
Qui d'autre sorte le conseille,
Soit pour ennemi réputé,
Car c'est de lui prêter l'oreille
Crime de lèse-majesté.

[2:194-97] (7)

It becomes clear that a few word changes can significantly alter the rigidities of Céladon's code. Of course, such a facile transformation is reciprocal: Hylas's twelve laws are just as readily converted back to Céladon's! But perhaps that is the point: each "system," as postulated by Céladon and Hylas, is never anything more than a set of laws, than language. (It is never a question of whose system "works." Hylas and his ways are clearly more integrated into L'Astrée, the romance, than are those of Céladon and Silvandre, for whom there is an enormous gap between ideals and what happens to them. But the romance Hylas artfully weaves is not an example of a reality principle per se. Rather, what "happens" in the novel to Hylas may be viewed as the libidinal projection of a narcissistic male, psychologically determined to secure all women for himself.) The Codes do not operate on a so-called "real" level: they are mental constructs which create and are in turn nourished wholly by language. As such, both Céladon's laws and Hylas's laws are texts unto themselves, articulations of other texts, past and future, in short, of two opposing, but never resolved, intellectual constructs. Above all else, both sets of laws are firmly literary: it is not surprising that they appear as poems, for the verse format allows their true literariness, and their ultimate debt to other texts, to surface.

Conclusion

The ideological claims which buttress L'Astrée are severely undermined by a tense, chilling atmosphere, the result of essential insecurity and imposed societal rigidity. At the same time, Hylas's relativistic, freedom-oriented views—and the stories which interpret them—work to reduce the inflexible, repressive ideas conveyed by the philosopher-intellectuals of L'Astrée. Into the tight, claustrophobic world where abstractions predominate over life, the narrative interjects flagrant denials: the libidinal projections of the male which nullify the posture of the idealized "perfect" lover. Violently aggressive for Childéric and Gondebaud, such fantasies are tempered, their brutality neutralized by the freedom based thinking and actions of Hylas.

Chapter Six
Disguise: From Travesty to Transvestism

When Céladon becomes Alexis, d'Urfé's novel acquires the titillating liveliness of the best romance. The many pages devoted to the cohabitation of Astrée and Alexis-Céladon are also among the book's most brilliant, as d'Urfé first adapts and then extends traditions culled from pastoral and baroque literature. Disguise in L'Astrée, of course, was no mere exercise in literary fidelity, although the very conventionality of the technique is apparent from a comparison to Spanish and Italian pastoral works, as well as to Elizabethan drama. Moreover, travesty as a significant literary technique continued to influence French writers who followed d'Urfé: Corneille, for example, in his comedies, as well as Gomberville. Edward Baron Turk maintains in his study of Gomberville's Polexandre that "romanesque conventions themselves . . . tend to promote frequent transvestism in the name of disguise" (1). Thus, while the various taboos and obstacles which impede amorous union, and which are the source of romance, force the protagonists to adopt strategies that will allow for the viability of the couple, disguise has a function beyond the mere level of permitting approach toward the loved one, or, alternately, escape from a rapacious predator. In the novels of the age, travesty quickly becomes transvestism, and eroticism, seemingly alien to pastoral mores, thereby erupts in the text, through subterfuge that occurs both in the diegesis as well as in acts described there. And although such seeming "irregularities" are ultimately corrected, their role throughout L'Astrée is predominant, while resolution offers only a quick bow to sexual, moral, and literary order.

D'Urfé's novel lies on a foundation of disguise. From the earliest pages, and at repeated intervals throughout his four parts, the author of L'Astrée reminds everyone (characters and readers, alike) that the shepherds and shepherdesses of Forez are not so by birth. Rather, they are the descendants of knights and their ladies who chose to abandon the conflicted, political

world of the court for the so-called bliss of country
life. (That life in Forez is far from blissful, that the
tyrant Love destroyed all hopes for a tranquil haven, has
been shown elsewhere in this volume.) Such essential
disguise enjoyed a solid tradition in pastoral literature, particularly in the Spanish works which influenced
d'Urfé (2).

But this transformation from one social order to
another, once accomplished, is not a functional aspect of
the plot's movement, except insofar as it helps to explain "intuitive" bravery and generosity. D'Urfé repeatedly recalls for his readers the noble lineage of the
shepherds and shepherdesses in order to counteract a
"popular" orientation, anathema no doubt to the aristocratic audience who would determine the novel's success.
But as an operable force such disguise has little power
in L'Astrée, and is significant only at the Battle of
Marcilly, where Céladon's bravery, in particular, be-
speaks a "gene" for soldiering!

Sexual disguise, on the other hand, prevalent throughout L'Astrée, allows for the diverse plots to advance
while creating a rarified romanesque atmosphere at anti-
podes from "reality." By sexual disguise, I refer to
those situations where gender is concealed beyond a
momentary, tactical level. There are, of course, also
countless examples of essentially tactical disguise in
the book. Typically, one character puts on the clothing
of another who is of the same or different sex. Even
when the disguise crosses sexual boundaries and is therefore rich in potential erotic behavior, some masquerades
are more "tactical" than others. Thus, Silviane pretends
to be a man, in order to escape from Childéric, following a pattern typical of the "roman d'aventures"; and
Mélandre, in order to be near her lover, Lydias, dons
male garb and is commonly considered to be a man. But,
as Maxime Gaume has correctly shown, these shifts are
momentary ones, tactical in nature, rarely opening onto
the larger vista of sexual play (3).

Although there are several examples of significant,
successful disguise in d'Urfé's book, I have chosen to
focus on three among them: the Diane-Filandre episode,
which includes several subdisguises within the principal
masquerade; the Diane-Phillis-Silvandre story, whereby
Phillis, a female, and Silvandre, a male, engage in a
competition to win Diane's affection; and finally, the
Alexis-Astrée tale (which is part of a general pattern

whereby Céladon is dressed as a girl), spanning three
volumes, and unquestionably the most evocative and provocative disguise episode of L'Astrée. Structurally,
the first and third episodes share much in common, with
disguise the means for the male to approach a reluctant
female. The narrative which describes the wooing of
Diane by Phillis and Silvandre differs from the other two
in that Phillis remains physically undisguised. Her
femaleness is not relinquished, even in travesty. Ostensibly, this episode is a charade: can Phillis successfully mimic male, "courtois" behavior, based on service?

Nonetheless, despite these differences, all three
episodes offer a similar premise—sexual inversion—which
d'Urfé deftly twists and turns to create multiple, even
dizzying meanings, simultaneously. Through a fundamental
convention of Neoplatonic thought, he is able to establish a socially sanctioned pattern that is nonetheless
easily, but radically, altered into a confusing sexual
situation. Because of the high investment Neoplatonism
placed on friendship, close bonds between women were
socially accepted and encouraged, free of the stigma
relative to the modern era. D'Urfé's writing adheres to
this tradition by portraying intensely rich emotional
links between women, in a world where the male is often a
greedy predator. Female attachments thrive in L'Astrée, always free of the sexual power base which viti-
ates heterosexual relationships, for they are a relief
from the radically unstable universe of the couple. Free
of doubt and suspicion, bonds among women seem transparent and innocent, conveying no recrimination or bitterness, but only trust and genuine communication.

Yet, the charms of female bonding are not at the heart
of d'Urfé's novel. Rather, he uses the convention of
female friendship to develop a textual experiment whereby
awareness of both heterosexuality and homosexuality
simultaneously filter into the reader's mind, only to
dissolve into an essential sexuality entirely independent
of gender. Some may object here that our mores are not
those of the seventeenth century, even less so of the
fifth century, and that it is only the modern mind which
seeks out a homosexual pattern where d'Urfé intended
none. It is therefore important to be clear: Honoré
d'Urfé's intent was not to portray lesbianism along with
heterosexual union, weighing the value of one against the
other. What he does seek to realize, and quite successfully, is erotic writing which intimates both forms of

loving while denying the signal importance of either. Here, textuality is sexuality, and both gender and character fade before the unyielding voice of desire and obstacle.

Despite centuries of devotion to Céladon, the poet, and to Astrée, the perfect mistress, readers have always recognized the prurient nature of d'Urfé's book, or at least of certain passages. Both Boileau and Huet sharply criticized the atmosphere of L'Astrée. But despite critical needs focusing on the "serious" side of the work, on its moral philosophy, generations of readers have appreciated the passages of sexual inversion. They are not only fun to read; for the critic they offer a remarkable example of an eroticism generated through a cleverly constructed diegesis.

The Diane-Filandre Episode

To keep track of all this narrative's characters and relationships is in itself a remarkable feat! Recounted by Diane, in an attempt to explain her past, the episode loses its readers in a labyrinth of inverse sexual relationships. These machinations and masquerades are narrated blithely by Diane, who, as much as any other "voice" in d'Urfé's novel, accepts premises wholly beyond what is normally typed as "reality." But to insist that the tale seems "unrealistic" is to deny d'Urfé's deliberate effort at creating a self-contained, self-referential world. Accepting the idea that fiction is inherently false, Honoré d'Urfé stretches this premise to the limit. The tale that Diane narrates is patently absurd, if examined from a "real" perspective; but it is vastly amusing if accepted as essential fiction, as a fantastic delirium of words.

Diane's parents, before her birth, vowed that their child would marry the offspring of Phormion and his wife. But both families produce girls! Diane's father dies before she is born, and avaricious Phormion, eager to acquire her wealth, decides to disguise his own daughter as a boy, in order to ensure a match. Called Filidias, "she" is raised as a shepherd. Phormion's goal is to obtain Diane's riches through a phony alliance between the two children, and then, when she is of age, to wed her to his nephew, Amidor. When Phormion dies, Diane's fate is scarcely improved, for Filidias decides to remain

"male" (thereby preserving the greater liberty she has
come to prize), and maintains Diane, who is her alibi, as
a virtual prisoner.

This unhappy situation, based on a permanent sexual
inversion which therefore is particularly threatening to
Diane, is interrupted by the arrival of Callirée and her
brother, Filandre, whose coincidence of name with Diane's
"master" can scarcely be overlooked. It is a sign that
both will sustain a similar fate, in this instance transvestism. Diane, along with her friend Daphnis, who is
Callirée's relative, spend much happy time with the newly arrived brother and sister. Filandre falls in love
with Diane, not without arousing the jealousy of Phormion's nephew, Amidor, who desires her for himself. The
friendly "salon" composed of Diane, Daphnis, Filandre,
and Callirée typically spends much time conversing,
composing, and singing. One favorite theme is the close,
often loving relationships between women, represented
here in a madrigal from Diane to Daphnis.

> Pourquoi semble-t-il tant étrange,
> Que fille comme vous étant,
> Toutefois je vous aime tant?
> Si l'amant en l'aimé se change,
> Ne puis-je pas mieux me changer,
> Etant bergère en vous bergère?
> Qu'étant bergère en un berger?
>
> > [1:202]
>
> Why does it seem so strange,
> That although you are a girl
> I love you so?
> If the lover is transformed into the beloved,
> Can I a shepherdess not be more easily transformed
> Into a shepherdess
> Than into a shepherd?

Such madrigals in this narrative are no mere bow to
Neoplatonic convention, but are rather a literary prelude
to the breach of heterosexuality which ultimately occurs.
Diane will accept Filandre's friendship, but not his
love, until he and his sister change places, each pretending to be the other. Once Filandre is transformed into
Callirée, Diane will accept from "her" the most ardent
professions of amorous faith, and will, in return, extend
her moves to include highly suggestive intimacies: "As
for us, when we had been left alone, Daphnis and I

caressed Filandre [that is, Callirée] as is customary
among women, I mean among those where there is friendship
and closeness, all of which this shepherd received and
reciprocated with so much feeling . . ." [1:212]. This
intimacy has distinct repercussions in the larger circle.
Seeing the closeness between Filandre-Callirée and
Diane, Daphnis reveals that she, too, loves Diane, and
she assumes henceforth a voyeuristic stance, titillated
by Diane's new relationship. Meanwhile, Filandre-
Callirée needs little encouragement to continue his
courtship of Diane, as the latter explains, charging her
narrative now with the feminine pronoun: "she experienced no problem in speaking freely of her passion to me,
but nonetheless as a woman. And because she swore that
she was feeling the same emotions and passions as men
when they are in love, and it was a great relief to
describe them; and because we were often alone, and did
not find such conversation disagreeable, she would kneel
before me to convey her true affection, and Daphnis, who
enjoyed all this, sometimes encouraged her" [1:214].
D'Urfé has created here a fascinating contradiction.
While maintaining that such talk is like that of a woman,
he paints a stereotypically "courtois" scene of declaration, a perfect mime of heterosexual courtship rites. In
the reader's mind, a male posture emerges, despite the
textual disclaimer of womanly talk, and then takes over,
submerging female friendship beneath heterosexual coupling.

Having established his basic pattern of inversion,
d'Urfé then multiplies the examples of travesty gone
haywire. Nephew Amidor, once promised for Diane, now
falls in love with "Callirée," that is, with the real
Filandre, a boy. Filidias, the woman disguised as a man
to whom Diane was supposedly "wed" as a child, falls in
love with "Filandre," that is, with the real Callirée, a
girl. Comments d'Urfé beguilingly: "Look how mad is
Love, and how he spends his time! He makes Filidias,
who's a girl, love a girl, and Amidor [love] a man . . ."
[1:212]. But this subterfuge of narrative naiveté fails
to conceal the obvious goal of inverted coupling ad
infinitum.

There is surely a playful intent to such writing: how
many couples may be formed among a given set of characters? How many sexual transformations may occur, all
violating the most generous reality principle, but all
adhering to the wholly fictional premises of a novel? In

the Filandre-Callirée episode, with its prelude of
Filidias, no one ever suspects the diverse ruses. Tone
of voice, facial characteristics, body form, nothing
belies the masquerade, for it is not the goal of d'Urfé
to persuade his readers of the narrative's veracity. Conventionally and obviously fantastic, such travesty is the
essence of the romanesque, proclaiming literature as
play.

Nonetheless, behind such gaming in L'Astrée lies
the distinct fear of heterosexual love, which was discussed earlier in the present volume. It is clear from
the Diane-Filandre episode that Diane rejects the male,
but not male courtship patterns if they proceed from a
perceived female! Indeed, any statement may be uttered,
any caress granted and exchanged, since Diane firmly
believes that Filandre is his sister Callirée. The most
equivocal play with the presumption of female involvement
seems entirely tolerable, even desirable, while with a
known male even preliminary verbal overtures are frequently rebuffed. Such a distinction must therefore be based
on a rather specific fear, or fears. In L'Astrée
there is a predominant phobic reaction toward the male,
based on fear of betrayal, and, behind that, of the
phallus. Astrée's dream, discussed later, confirms the
presence of such apprehension, and is one more indication
of female retreat in the face of heterosexuality. Simi-
larly, Diane's reputed "coldness," evident in both the
Filandre and Silvandre episodes (name similarity once
more establishing situational identity), is merely the
outer manifestation of the inner anxiety.

In this instance, however, fear of heterosexual involvement does not open onto a field of pure eroticism,
free of gender, as it will in the Astrée-Alexis episode.
Transvestism is effectively blocked here by the narrative voice which maintains the characters in their essential identity, even while allowing for convincing
masquerades. Thus, Filandre, despite his cosmetic transformation into a girl, is still referred to as Filandre,
or, alternately, as "la feinte Callirée," thereby maintaining an unblemished picture of maleness in the
reader's mind. Only irregularly is the disguised
Filandre referred to as "she," and when such narrative
transformation of the pronoun does occur, it is at
moments of speech rather than of act. Behind the mask,
therefore, we constantly glimpse the "true" self, and
thus, the true sex.

Nor do the male-male (Amidor-Filandre) or female-female (Filidias-Callirée) couples ever really convey homosexual bonding. Attractions are there, it is true, but the narrator maintains these "as if" they were based on opposite sex magnetism. Amidor desires Callirée, or the female disguised side of Filandre, rendering anodyne the potential male-male attraction. The narrative itself persistently blocks any other connotation from surfacing, with the exception perhaps of Daphnis's attraction to Diane, which develops and thrives in an atmosphere of third-party, voyeuristic participation.

In short, and despite d'Urfé's flirtation here with a polyvalent eroticism, this episode declines to assume the full possibilities inherent to a transvestite situation. Aside from the earlier mentioned scene of caresses among Diane, Daphnis, and "Filandre disguised as Callirée," there are scarcely any acts which would generate a sexually charged atmosphere. Unlike the Alexis-Astrée tale, this narrative retreats from the silence of true sexuality and exists almost entirely in the word. Thus, the various partners in their disguised, sham states, articulate a genuine language, germane to their essential identity, but which is nonetheless not received as such since costume has concealed essence. Such pastime fails to open onto a larger world of sexual play, held in check by a narration that focuses on "courtois" patterns, and particularly on discourse. There is almost no touching or even voyeuristic seeing in this episode (again, Daphnis is the exception), which remains fixed in language. And precisely because no sexually subversive act has occurred, precisely because nudity has not surfaced and penetrated the text, Diane is able to forgive Filandre his ruse. Their happiness is negated not by the continued refusal to unite as a couple (as will be the case with Astrée), but by Filandre's untimely death. With this episode, Honoré d'Urfé tantalizingly creates the potential for a dramatic eroticism based on projections and fantasies, but stops short of assuming the full implications of this potentially explosive situation.

Diane-Silvandre-Phillis Episode

The name patterning which d'Urfé uses to convey repetition and/or lack of individuation, and which occurs between Filandre and Silvandre, narratively suggests that

Diane will be trapped again in an episode of disguise.
Indeed, when Silvandre and Phillis, on a wager, compete
to serve best Diane's interests, the "cold" shepherdess
is once more drawn into a masquerade where her favors are
supposedly the desired goal. But d'Urfé hardly repeats
the Filandre-Filidias episode. This time he chooses a
dramatically different type of travesty, equally suggestive but more puzzling. "As if" seems somehow less playful here, perhaps because the mechanism of disguise is no
longer a change of clothes and thus appears more essential, closer to the authentic self. Yet, in this episode, too, d'Urfé carefully disallows overt eroticism,
skirting it always but without creating the explosive
power of the Alexis story. Here, d'Urfé's text seems an
experiment in creating, and then restricting eroticism,
through narrative means.

In the second volume we are informed of the peculiar
wager that has occurred. Quarreling playfully, Phillis
challenges Silvandre to serve a shepherdess in order to
prove his untested worth. He accepts on the condition
that Phillis do the same. The result of this mutual
challenge is that both will serve Diane, who in three
months time will decide which character is more love-
worthy. This odd situation works at the conventional
level, as it did in the Filandre episode, for intensely
close friendships between women are permissible under
Renaissance Platonic doctrine. Nonetheless, such
doctrine cannot completely displace the inherently
strange situation of a female assuming a male-oriented,
"courtois" posture. Nor does d'Urfé appear to wish to
deny the strangeness of the wager. Phillis, he tells us
quickly, "knew so well how to feign a woman ardently in
love ["la passionnée"] that no shepherd could have come
off any better" [2:293]. It is the curious word inter-
change of "la passionnée" with "le berger" in the original that allows for the immediately suggestive sexual
inversion to surface in the reader's mind, even as yet
only a glimmer.

In this episode, two separate layers of fiction are
prominent. The first—Silvandre really does fall in love
with Diane, thereby rendering his sham an act of genuine
faith—is less puzzling as a narrative exercise. His
disguise, which assumes the form of pretending to woo
Diane through services, quickly meshes with a level of
(textual) reality, as he falls in love for the first time
in his life. Reticent in declaring himself outside the

level of travesty, Silvandre delays hearing Diane's expected judgment, which will determine whether he himself or
Phillis is the better suitor. Silvandre reasons that if
the fiction ends, so, too, will the corresponding reality. Thus, his whole behavioral pattern is simultaneously
disguise and truth, for his imitation of a lover has been
transformed into an essential truth. Where subterfuge
ends and so-called reality (that is, within the premises
of this wholly fictional undertaking) takes over, cannot
be determined, for they are virtually identical, the one
creating, engendering the other. Furthermore, there are
clear advantages for Diane in allowing the travesty to
continue. In an ironic blending of tales, Céladon,
disguised as Alexis, counsels Diane to permit Silvandre's
sham, for it is inherently less threatening than "reality," and, as an important extra measure, is accepted by
society: "Let him continue the strategy he has utilized
up until now, and since such an acceptance will offer him
the means to avoid his true passion, the flame will
consequently be less intense; and, if by chance, it
flares up and becomes visible, this won't seem so unusual
because everyone is already accustomed to it" [3:562].
In this instance, disguise becomes a desirable stance
negating the potential for a true explosion of sexuality
that the undisguised and therefore unrestrained self
might release. As such, travesty is the ultimate sublimation, coveted by both actor and spectator, a playacting
eroticism sanctioned by the prevailing social currents.

Such disguise, when it mimics sex play, is a significant element in the whole system of sublimation that
L'Astrée establishes and then assumes almost emblemati-
cally. But it is less structurally open than the more
common masquerade based on sexual inversion. The identity between Silvandre's feigned love and his subsequent
real love is a fascinating orchestration; it is nonetheless limited in its erotic potential. On the other
hand, the second level of "play" in this episode, involving Phillis, is by its very nature a more imaginative
situation. To the letter, Phillis successfully duplicates male-typed "courtois" behavior, while merely
intensifying, in appearance at least, the convention of
female friendship. How one reads this episode, which
perspective one adopts, will determine the thrust of the
narrative. Such an option, however, clear as it appears,
may not really exist, for the reader is forced into a
double, simultaneous perspective, which, vacillating

between a "male" and "female" bond, allows for a polyvalent relationship to surface.

Phillis's play exists strictly on the level of word
and service. A mime of chivalric comportment, her actions
and language mirror perfectly the traditional male in
service to his mistress: Phillis, for example, endearing-
ly refers to Diane as "ma maîtresse" throughout the
episode. There is no physical disguise here. Phillis
appears visibly female to all, and it is this nondisguised state, precisely, which jolts the reader who
"hears" male-linked language and who "sees" male-typed
acts. Diane, moreover, reciprocates this travesty,
extending to the distinctly female Phillis reactions more
in keeping with heterosexual courtship. Throughout
L'Astrée, fetishes abound, themselves forms of sublimated love, "stand-ins" for the denied presence of the
beloved. Ribbons, hats, all articles of clothing, are
cherished and caressed, kept close to the body, and are
identified absolutely with the desired person. Astrée
and Céladon's relationship, in particular, is filled
with such fetish objects, whose erotic base d'Urfé
scarcely conceals. Duplicating the atmosphere of that
narrative, Diane and Phillis's tale, too, allows for the
erotic representation of the body through fetishes.
Diane makes bracelets out of her hair—just as Astrée
had done for Céladon—which she offers to Phillis, thereby provoking Silvandre's jealousy. Once more, convention
(both social and literary) allows for an "innocent" interpretation. The offering of a gift to a dear friend may
be acceptable within the confines of the Neoplatonic
code, and Diane's presenting hair bracelets to Phillis
may be viewed in this light. Nonetheless, Phillis in
this narrative is miming male comportment, and thus the
hair bracelet assumes a more sexual dimension, as an
extension of Diane's person. Moreover, the fact that
Astrée had presented such articles to Céladon establishes a clear heterosexual model. Yet, at the same time,
since Phillis has not disguised herself physically, her
femaleness is still apparent to the reader: the name is
Phillis; the pronouns are female. Thus, the act, linked
initially to love as well as to friendship, assumes here
additionally (but without canceling the "courtois" model)
a homosexual connotation. All three levels—female
friendship, heterosexual courtship, homosexual relationship—coexist in the narrative, none allowed to come to
fruition, but none denied textual status. Nor does one

level predominate; it is, rather, their simultaneous
intermingling which creates a puzzling, but tantalizing
perspective for the reader.

Words match gifts. Léonide, explaining to others the
complicated ruse, admits that Phillis's behavior corre-
sponds perfectly to that of a shepherd. Both her actions
and language are the ideal mime of male-linked courtship
patterns:

> You have noticed perhaps . . . that Silvandre and
> Phillis call Diane their mistress, and that they serve
> her and perform duties which all shepherds who see her
> must perform, [because of] her great beauty and worth.
> And while doubtless you will not have found it odd
> that this young shepherd, whose intelligence and good
> judgment you have noticed, loves and serves so beauti-
> ful and lovable a shepherdess as Diane, I would like
> to think that you will have been surprised to see that
> Phillis, who is a shepherdess, serves her as if she
> were a shepherd; and directs toward her the same words
> and the same acts that the most burning passion can
> produce in the heart of the most deeply affected
> lover; for it is not customary to see a girl serve
> another with such involvement. [3:498-99]

This remarkable passage is abruptly curtailed, as
Léonide resumes discussing other, less tantalizing
aspects of the masquerade; but the effect is startling,
for the brevity of the passage highlights the peculiar
"match." What troubles is the "as if," which is the grammatical and the narrative unit commanding the principal
disguise episodes of L'Astrée. In d'Urfé's novel,
"as if" tends to lose its hypothetical base, and to
convey a posture strikingly close to genuine inversion.
But it never does assume the totality of these erotic
possibilities, vacillating throughout the novel, suspended between the twin poles of disguise and essence.
Homosexuality certainly surfaces here, penetrating the
reader's mind if only subliminally, through d'Urfé's
manipulation of diverse narrative strategies. But no
overtly erotic act occurs. We shall never know if
Phillis is only feigning. Nor does it matter, for it is
not homosexuality or heterosexuality per se which is at
issue in L'Astrée. Rather, it appears that d'Urfé
was experimenting with the limits of his prose, striving
for that point in writing where a pure eroticism, inde

pendent of sexual distinction and of act, might be generated.

Once more, however, d'Urfé controls and restrains. What is created through the narrative is then abruptly restricted. As in the Filandre episode, the bulk of the courtship depends on verbal communication. What acts do occur reflect the service mandated by "la courtoisie," but they never transcend that. Even the one obvious sexual gesture, the offering by Diane of a hair bracelet, is reduced by its fetishistic, and therefore sublimated, status. Ultimately, it is precisely the refusal to interject the body obviously into his narrative that allows for the restraint of d'Urfé's text. Its absence is significant, for without the body's clear presence, textual sexuality can go only so far. Finally, sex play is abbreviated again in this tale, for at the moment Diane renders her judgment, however equivocal it is ("We say and declare that truly Phillis is more lovable than Silvandre, and that Silvandre knows better than Phillis how to make one love him" [3:520]), the characters resume their habitual identity. The whole episode thus appears as an interlude, a game between games, a fiction among all the others, as a brief moment of identity gone awry, perhaps revealing all, but perhaps not.

Céladon-Astrée Episodes

Three separate episodes portray Céladon dressed up and disguised as a female. While each has a purely tactical goal at its base, the first and third chronologically (as regards narrated time) also open onto the field of sexual play and transvestism, while the second, concerning Céladon's escape from Galathée's palace, remains confined to the level of strategic disguise.

"LUCINDE." When, in an effort to flee the palace of Isoure, Céladon is transformed into Lucinde, a relative of Adamas, disguise is only momentary and declines to expand into sexual games (for Astrée is absent). Thus, the Lucinde episode is significant primarily because it reveals how easily Céladon masquerades as a woman. In terms of plot, this will make the Alexis episode less startling (for even within the extreme fictional limits of L'Astrée, the Alexis episode is unique), as we slowly adapt ourselves to Céladon's femaleness, as we accept the premise that he is a convin-

cing girl! Honoré d'Urfé, however, rarely uses such a
significant tactic as a means solely to advance plot. In
this instance, even the highly conventional Lucinde
episode focuses the reader's attention on the fact that
for a significant portion of L'Astrée, Céladon appears as a woman. Such femalizing implies conversely the
de-masculinizing of the protagonist, and Céladon is in
fact most successful in his efforts to woo Astrée when,
precisely, he is disguised as a woman. Dressed up,
Céladon subjugates Astrée, but only then. As was the
case for Diane in the Filandre episode, Astrée will
accept the most ardent love expressions and acts from
Céladon, provided that the latter is disguised as a
girl. When he is released from this travesty, she
rejects him: effectively, it is his maleness that she is
banishing.

The Lucinde episode, momentary and tactical in its
fundamental goal of permitting escape from Galathée, is
thus emblematic of Céladon's basic posture throughout
L'Astrée. While avoiding an erotic base, this passage
nonetheless establishes Céladon as a female presence;
and, coincidentally, this occurs on the recommendation of
Adamas, whose relative "Lucinde" purportedly is, thereby
creating a precedent for the Alexis episode, which also
results from the conniving of Adamas.

"ORITHIE." Not surprisingly, this episode is the
genesis of the entire Astrée-Céladon relationship,
fixing it forever under the sign of disguise. Perhaps
even more than the Alexis episode, which is long and
drawn out, really a series of episodes, the Orithie
passage is the best known segment of L'Astrée. It is
also the most troubling episode for those who seek to
label the novel as Neoplatonic or "précieux." Speaking
with a sense of shame and embarrassment, yet with some
pleasure as well, Astrée relates to her friends Diane
and Phillis how Céladon was able to establish their
relationship. Rebuffed by her in his nondisguised, male
state, Céladon transforms himself into Orithie, a girl.
"She," in turn, is assuming the role of Pâris in a celebration that mimics ancient Greek rites, whereby an apple
is granted the woman he judges to be the most beautiful.
The risks are enormous, for in past years other men have
crept in among the shepherdesses to observe them nude.
Now it is ordered that anyone who commits such a crime
will be stoned.

A curious, confused state of affairs indeed! Céladon

is dressed up as Orithie, a would-be female who is assuming the role of a male, Pâris. The intervention of a female persona allows for Céladon to fulfill the original thrust of the Greek story: Pâris's judgment.   But how are we to read the scene?   Explicitly sexual, the tableau portrays a naked Astrée covered only by her long hair and a garland of flowers that Céladon had given her the day before. Such unchecked voyeurism is hardly original to d'Urfé. Earlier pastoral fiction, particularly the Italian works, had allowed for "spy" scenes with an erotic base: typically the lover watches his beloved while she bathes or sleeps.   D'Urfé's work is intriguing, however, not just for its adept, but nonetheless conventional use of voyeuristic scenes.   His originality, his brilliance, lie in having exploited the impossibility (for the reader at least) of relating sexuality to gender. Despite the presumed identity of "Orithie" as a female, Astrée is deeply embarrassed by the exposure of her naked self.   It may be assumed that she suspects, subconsciously at least, a ruse; but there is nothing in the written text which states this.   Rather, the episode is troubling precisely because of its veiled, and doubly charged, sexuality.   If "Orithie" is "read" by Astrée to be a girl, the convention of close female friendship assumes a curious coloration, all the more so in that Astrée is, and perceives herself to be, disturbed. The form becomes not mere friendship, but something more, or something else.   It skirts lesbianism.   If, on the other hand, she perceives, even subconsciously, Céladon behind the mask, a voyeuristic sexuality surfaces, pleasurable to both onlooker and victim, in full denial of the metaphysical speculation which reputedly governs the novel. At the very least, the allusion to nudity negates the notion of female bonding free of sexuality and encourages the reader's own sense of titillation, to say nothing of that of Céladon and Astrée.   The dizzying, confusing levels of lies—Céladon feigning Orithie, who is miming Pâris—and all simultaneously experienced by the reader, work to cancel a specific, gender-typed sexuality, in favor of an eroticism at the "zero degree."   Any effort to separate and compartmentalize is doomed to failure: d'Urfé intends for a polyvalent sexuality to emerge from his text.   Yet, despite the evident play that is generated in this passage, its brevity hinders any further exploration of this absolute, textually created eroticism. With the Alexis narrative, however, d'Urfé strengthens his textual play.

THE ALEXIS-ASTREE NARRATIVE.   The ready acceptance of this episode, an acceptance that is Astrée's as
well as ours, is based on the convention of desexualized
female friendship, as are all the significant disguise
episodes of the novel.   (It is based also on our familiarity with Céladon "in drag.")   A double freedom is
implied, both corollaries of the masquerade premise.   All
words and acts (which, obviously, stop short of sexual
consummation) are socially acceptable if female relating
is implied; but the same word or gesture, in short, the
same sign, is rejected if heterosexuality is the govern-
ing pattern.   A psychological freedom permeates the text
as well, for once the threat of heterosexual coupling is
removed, the female comfortably participates in the most
intimate duos.

     To a large extent, the Alexis episode repeats and
strengthens the disguise motif of earlier narratives.   On
the advice of Adamas, once more, Céladon is persuaded to
disguise himself as Alexis, daughter to the great druid
himself.   The real Alexis has been absent for eight
years, since she is a druidic princess and resides with
others of the sect.   Adamas's plan is ingeniously simple,
as he explains to Céladon: "Perhaps you recall I told
you that there is considerable resemblance—in both age
and appearance—between you two.   Thus I will spread the
rumor that she has been ill for some time and that the
ancient druids are of the opinion that I withdraw
her until such time as she is well enough to perform the
required exercises.   A few days later you will dress up
like her, and I will receive you under the name of
Alexis, my daughter . . ." [2:397].   Céladon, who passionately desires to be near Astrée, nonetheless wonders how
he will manage this without countering Astrée's law that
stipulates she never see him until she herself orders it.
Adamas's casuistry—not surprising in a character who
does as much matchmaking as moralizing—is, however,
persuasive.   To Céladon's statement that however disguised, he is still Céladon, and thus in disobedience to
Astrée's orders, Adamas replies: "That you are
Céladon, there is no doubt, . . . but it is not because
of this that you will defy her order, for she didn't
command you to cease being Céladon, but only to cease
showing her this Céladon.   And she will not be seeing
you, but Alexis.   In conclusion, if she doesn't know you,
you will not offend her; if she does recognize you and
becomes angry, you can hope only for death.   And wouldn't
such an end be preferable to languishing in this fash-

ion?" [2:398]. In short, Adamas connives, and Céladon
accepts, to maintain the letter of Astrée's law, while
flagrantly violating its spirit. The "perfect lover"
thus enters into a situation of ill-concealed voyeurism,
where libidinal fantasies of the most blatantly erotic
sort may readily be sustained.

The Alexis-Astrée episode, which begins in part 2 and
continues through part 4, duplicates and extends the
sense of a world gone awry that was first glimpsed in the
Filandre-Silvandre-Diane episodes. Significantly,
language here intimates two levels of relating, as does
costume. The long conversations between Alexis and
Astrée, with their obvious "courtois" (some might say
"précieux") overtones, duplicate the habitual expression
of heterosexual courtship, and yet also transfer such
language to bonding between females. The masquerade,
viewed literally, is at least marginally suggestive of a
homosexual relationship, as the creation of Alexis under-
mines and negates the codified, stereotypical male
language (4); or perhaps does not negate, but rather
joins it, forming thereby a double and simultaneous
image. The teasing thrust of homosexuality, always skirting the text, is brought home humorously, moreover, when
the ardent womanizer, Hylas, falls passionately in love
with Alexis-Céladon, thus helping to preserve the sense
of folly which permeates L'Astrée during these labyrinthine exercises in travesty.

Where the Alexis episode assumes a markedly different
tone, however, from the Filandre-Silvandre sections is in
its obvious introduction of nudity. In the episodes
involving Diane, disguise was essentially dependent on
the adept use of "courtois" language. The lengthy Alexis
passages, however, extend the voyeuristic, erotic base of
the Orithie episode, curtailed before a full adventure
could commence. In the sections which recount Céladon's
metamorphosis into Alexis, the body, and particularly the
seminude body, is everywhere, a flaunting tease to Neoplatonic bonds. The convention of female friendship, too,
is stretched to its limit, moving beyond the level of
fetishism to one dependent on touching, caressing, and
kissing. The relationships between women are submerged
in an erotic atmosphere which no reader—whatever the era
or its mores—can ignore.

It is this close bonding between and among women, of
course, conventionally at the heart of L'Astrée, which
allows for the fundamental premise: Alexis-Céladon and

Astrée live side by side in a communal atmosphere. The
rites associated with sleep—dressing, undressing, brush-
ing of the hair, and letting it down—occupy a large
amount of time, all deliciously prolonged by Alexis.
"Her" relationship with Astrée, throughout the lengthy
episode, is held tantalizingly in suspense by d'Urfé,
who must maintain intact the polyvalent sexual experience
without breaching overtly the limitations imposed by
Platonic-type friendship. On one level, the articulated
one, all is correct: Astrée and Alexis enjoy the conventionally and socially sanctioned bond of woman-to-woman
friendship. On another, Alexis is really Céladon, thereby insinuating heterosexuality among the presumed female
friendship signs. And on yet another level, the signs
themselves are peculiarly [homo]sexualized, despite their
stated and accepted literary and social conventionality.
Caresses in the nude are erotic, no matter what the networks of convention may sanction, and they are all the
more so when a double experience is created. In this
perspective, a veiled lesbianism surfaces, free of any
stated moral stigma, it is true, but nonetheless titil-
latingly erotic.
    The entire Alexis episode is maintained through a
sexual suspense often deliberately equivocal and therefore all the more powerful, and which is always on the
verge of exploding. Astrée is undressed much of the
time, and is thus constantly exposed to the gaze of
Alexis-Céladon. Looking moves quickly to embracing as
Alexis "kissed first her eyes, then her mouth, and then
her breast, while the shepherdess made no objection,
believing her to be a girl" [3:598]—and such ardent
declarations of passion occur repeatedly throughout the
episode. The Alexis incident is an exploration of a
sexual fantasy, a dream where there is no "reality"
principle to tame it, and where only narrative intervention of a rhetorical nature—"Oh Love, how you enjoy
tormenting in so many different ways those who are your
followers" [3:550]—occasionally serves to dampen an
explosively sensual scene.
    In themselves, voyeuristic scenes such as these are
hardly original, appearing in both Spanish and Italian
pastorals. D'Urfé faithfully maintains the voyeurism,
but by converting the Céladon character into a female
character, Alexis, he doubles and thereby extends the
fantasy. From part 2 on, Céladon is referred to as
Alexis in those passages dependent primarily on act:

touches, kisses, embraces. Only when the character meditates on the peculiar predicament does d'Urfé allow him
his true appellation. Thus, subtly, Céladon becomes a
woman, through our reading of a female name. Behind this
mask, however, one still "feels" the presence of the male
character, despite the shift to the proper noun, Alexis,
which, far more than mere clothing disguise, intimates a
feminine identity. Such "maleness" becomes yet more
difficult to perceive, however, when not only names, but
pronouns as well are altered. "Elle" replaces "il,"
thereby insinuating homosexuality into the text via the
grammatical level. The passage cited above, when Alexis
kisses Astrée's body, and feminine pronouns proliferate,
conveys the intimate linking of identical gender through
grammar.

At the same time the story level, as opposed to the
grammatical one, maintains the presence of Céladon, a
male who is only disguised as Alexis. Both levels penetrate the reader's mind, where they coexist and where,
with only considerable difficulty, and in opposition to
the reading experience, they can be separated one from
the other. The result is that neither heterosexuality
nor homosexuality can predominate; instead, their coex-
istence allows them to cancel out each other, and for a
gender-free sexuality to emerge. In the end, sexual
identity, and hence identity itself, are lost in a maze
of pure eroticism.

But the loss of identity, which here entails loss of
characterization and therefore character, is not limited
to a situation depicting a simple (if radical) sexual
transformation. Not content to be merely "Alexis,"
Céladon orchestrates an elaborate fantasy whereby his
new persona strives for another transformation, this time
into Astrée herself. To be sure, the transformation of
self into the beloved, the joining of two souls such that
the lover is no longer properly himself, but wholly the
will of his mistress, these concepts Céladon had formulated in his Twelve Tables. Such union reflects the highly abstract idealism of Neoplatonism, but the application
of these ideals in tangible terms is remote. The union
praised by the Renaissance Platonists remains consistently cerebral, understood, but never functionally operable.
And it finds no space within the Astrée-Alexis narrative. Céladon's desire to "be" Astrée is a far cry
from the exalted spiritual union posited in the doctrinal
passages of d'Urfé's novel. As Céladon garbs himself in

Astrée's clothing, he is sensually aroused, and these feelings are duplicated when the shepherdess puts on "Alexis's" own vestments. It is here that d'Urfé's travesty moves rapidly toward transvestism. Waking up early one morning, Alexis mistakenly dons Astrée's dress, an error caused by the lack of daylight. Quickly, however, the act assumes a different, more deliberate quality, as Alexis-Céladon relishes the pleasure of this masquerade: "Love . . . produced enormous happiness in this false Alexis, from wearing the dress of her beloved shepherdess, so much so that unable to take it off, she began to kiss it and to press it affectionately against her body, and then, gazing on the table she saw her [Astrée's] head garments and the remainder of her outfit. Transported by love, she grabbed and kissed them, and put them on, and slowly became accustomed to wearing these clothes, to the point that anyone would have taken her for a shepherdess" [3: 593]. This rather extreme example of fetishism in fact negates the cerebral, abstract joining that is at the base of Neoplatonic thought. These are wholly erotic acts, whose sensual pleasure is not lost on Céladon.

The shepherd, moreover, is now doubly disguised, for Alexis has, through clothing, become Astrée! On one level, the female persona (Alexis) fades, even while d'Urfé maintains the feminine pronoun, for it is the image of Céladon-disguised-as-Astrée which surfaces and takes over. In this fashion, the heterosexual link is maintained. But throughout the episode d'Urfé carefully preserves the feminine pronoun, "elle," for both Alexis and Astrée, which allows for a lesbian level to coexist along with the more dominant heterosexual one. Finally, as Céladon is transformed into Astrée, and as such, gives up his identity for hers, the fantasy turns autoerotic, with no partner needed for its continuation. One figure alone caresses itself, the ultimate projection of sexual fulfillment in a solitary, and therefore completely nonthreatening, bond.

Yet, d'Urfé refuses to stop here. Having merged Astrée into Céladon-Alexis, having created a synthetic figure, he rejects even this form as a final statement. Dressed up as Astrée, whose clothing she has been kissing and stroking, Alexis "approached the bed where Astrée was sleeping, and kneeling down, began to worship her" [3:593]. Having been merged, the self now splits, as the figure and presence of Astrée are incarnated in

two separate entities, one, a composite figure of
Céladon, Alexis, and Astrée, who is voyeuristically
absorbed in watching the other, a sleeping girl. Who
desires whom? And what? Given the conventions of the
story, we know, or believe we know, the answer. But as
Honoré d'Urfé weaves his tale, the original Céladon-
Astrée link, which is the premise of the diegesis, is
wiped out, negated in favor of a character-free eroticism. Jacques Ehrmann, in an existential analysis of the
work, has focused precisely on this relational gap, which
creates in L'Astrée what he perceives to be an identity crisis. In a world without values, save the crushing
one of Love, the self withers, vacillates, and, finally,
is lost (5). Ehrmann's critical perspective is not without validity. Céladon in particular seems to undergo a
debilitating crisis, whereby he experiences a sense of
radical alienation from the social unit and from himself.
    Rather than a metaphysical identity crisis, however,
which seems oddly misplaced as regards d'Urfé's novel,
the scenes of travesty and transvestism reflect a double
goal. Identity as such is effectively denied, steady
characterization is canceled, just as Ehrmann suggests.
But this should come as no surprise in a work where
distinguishing, individual traits play only a small role,
if that. The self—either its physical or psychological
delineation—is never clearly painted in L'Astrée.
Names virtually duplicate themselves, as do situations.
Different characters experience similar, if not identical, events in their lives, with predictably parallel
results. Thus, while identity is effectively nullified
in the principal disguise episodes (as elsewhere in the
novel), it is not character or personality which is
denied, but rather gender. All the major disguise episodes occur in a potentially explosive sexual atmosphere;
and if identity vacillates, if the self is uprooted, it
is in reaction to the demands of sex.
    The fundamentally unstable situation depicted in these
episodes is thus not a mere reflection of an identity
crisis per se, not a simple indication of baroque forces
which might signal the loss of self. Identity has never
been sure in L'Astrée, where the characters are all
extensions of one another, variations on a theme. Instead, the easy movement of the self across gender, the
fusion of self into three figures (Céladon-Alexis-
Astrée), and the fission of a synthesized self into two
parts (Céladon "in drag," in Astrée's clothes, kneeling

before a sleeping, hence not-of-this-world Astrée), suggests a writing experience whose goal is the generation
of a pure eroticism, free of gender and character.
As hetero-, homo-, and auto-sexual levels coexist in an
erotic mass, the tension is all the greater, the fantasy
all the more potent. In an atmosphere where sexuality—
at least overt—is taboo, the text is nonetheless bathed
in it.

Yet, this remarkable disguise episode, where travesty
so wittingly becomes transvestism, is something more than
an experiment in writing, however rich in itself that may
be. The disguises which are never questioned and only
vaguely, if ever, grasped; the fusion and fission of com-
peting selves; the gender reversals—all point to a necessary sublimation on the part of Astrée. Earlier, I
discussed the paramount fear which governs the female
characters in d'Urfé's novel, a fear of betrayal which
ultimately conceals a more radical fear of heterosexuality. Céladon's disguise as Alexis, and even as herself,
Astrée, conveys the repression of the male figure under
a mask that is not only socially, but psychologically
acceptable as well. In truth, Céladon's disguise as
Alexis is governed by fear, too: fear that a revelation
of true identity will necessitate an immediate rupture.
At a moment of particular lucidity, speaking as Alexis,
he questions the whole masquerade, seeing it as a means
to maintain only an ambiguous desire and fear:

> [Céladon's] presence is as fearsome to me as it is
> desirable: desirable, because, without Céladon, I
> will never have perfect happiness, and fearsome,
> because only he can cause me to lose all hope.
> But when I want to return to myself, who am I, who
> fears and desires? Am I Alexis? No, because what can
> Alexis desire any further? Am I Céladon? No,
> because what can he fear who has attained the very
> pinnacle of misery? Who am I then, who desires and
> fears? For it is certain that I feel those two emo-
> tions. Without a doubt I am a combination of Alexis
> and Céladon, and thus, as Céladon, I desire to
> recoup the joy which was so unjustly snatched from me,
> and, as Alexis, I fear losing that which I now
> possess. Thus, I am Alexis and Céladon mixed
> together; but now that I know who I am, why not
> discover a way to content Céladon, and to reassure
> Alexis. [4:252]

It is this important passage, among others, which Ehrmann
points to as an indication of a metaphysical identity
crisis in a free-floating baroque world. And, in isolation, the words do convey a sense of alienation hardly
contrary to the atmosphere of L'Astrée, based on a
perceived loss of faith and on fear. Yet, while seemingly corroborating such an existential interpretation, the
passage also serves to expose the schizophrenic self that
lies at the heart of the entire episode. The fear which
Céladon describes is precisely that of losing intimacy
with Astrée, a state he realizes depends completely on
her sublimation of Céladon into Alexis. Céladon is
Alexis because Astrée's psychological peace depends on
his being so. In a sense, then, this fantasy is wholly
of Astrée's making, for it is she who creates the need,
subliminally in herself, consciously with Céladon, for
this elaborate disguise, whereby maleness is effectively
banished, at least as a sign.

Thus, while Céladon's perception of his fear remains
on a conscious level throughout the episode, as he joins
Astrée in the ruse, the shepherdess's anxiety consistently is subconscious, or at least subliminal. For the
relationship to function at all, Céladon must be a girl,
for it is only within the boundaries of this accepted
convention that Astrée will permit Céladon's advances.
Just as in the earlier disguise episodes involving Diane,
we can never be entirely sure what the characters' true
proclivities may be, and just as in those same passages
such a determination is ultimately irrelevant, in this
instance it is neither possible nor necessary to determine exactly what Astrée knows, or on what level. To the
contrary, for the tension generated by d'Urfé's writing
depends on her ambiguous psychological state: there
appears to be some glimmer of awareness, but it never
surfaces to the conscious level. When first "Alexis" and
Astrée encounter one another, a complex array of feelings instantly emerges, the embarrassment and lack of
control of both characters conveying the reality of all
passion: "Oh Love! to what state did you reduce them
when they ["elles"] kissed! The shepherdess blushed so,
as if her face were aflame, and Alexis, beside herself
with joy, began to tremble as if a sudden access of fever
had gripped her . . ." [3:66]. The narrator here is
describing an involuntary reaction—the mark of true
passion in seventeenth-century semiology—which is suggestive of a subliminal awareness on Astrée's part that

her encounter is with a Céladon-type figure. But such a
perception is never conscious on Astrée's part, nor is
there any narrative intervention on her behalf. Only her
redness signifies. And she retreats from developing
further her vague perception. It is as if "Alexis" becomes a projection in the shepherdess's mind, a safety
net for her psyche, whereby all will be permitted under
the sign of female bonding. Céladon cannot be permitted
to erupt in her mind's space, for maleness must be censored. Socially sanctioned, "Alexis" becomes a sublimated form of Céladon; and while the feminine pronoun
continues to jar readers, for Astrée such a shift to the
female form is eminently acceptable.

The newly created hybrid continues to function as a
split personality. Céladon is so named, and enjoys the
masculine pronoun whenever he meditates on his curious
situation. Even during the moments of sexual passion, he
retains his masculine identity as long as he is additionally perceived as a spectator to his own spectacle.
Unlike the earlier cited passage of sexual advance, where
Alexis is wholly "herself," the following section signals
a narrative shift, and the masculine pronoun is reintro-
duced: "The shepherdess, embarrassed, but eager to obey,
approaching Alexis dissolved in the arms of this shepherd
. . . Céladon would have liked to continue these caresses at length, but the considerations he had recently
formulated obliged him to hold back more than he would
have wished" [4:38]. In this fashion, d'Urfé withers
the homosexual allusion in favor of a strong heterosexual
one. In addition, the passage conveys the mental pro-
cesses, entirely Céladon's, and the physical ones, which
belong to both Céladon and Alexis. When there is an
absence of cognition in the text, the character appears
as uniquely feminine.

Such split nomenclature is common. In the above
citation, Alexis's name appears, followed by "the shepherd," and finally, by Céladon. The shift to heterosexual dominance is achieved strictly through linguistic
means. Elsewhere, such a division serves to indicate the
schizophrenic self: "Léonide [who is knowledgeable
regarding the ruse] was afraid that the habitual depression of Céladon would cause Alexis to formulate some new
plan" [3:556]. The narrative shift reflects not merely
Céladon's double role—and Léonide's understanding of
it—but on another level, Astrée's own need for such a
division. Her mind is fully prepared to accept the

Alexis persona; indeed, she seeks it, perhaps even creates it, for the story is a fantasy, although whose is never clear. As in Buñuel's film Belle de Jour, we are never sure if the erotic projection is the wife's or the "boy scout" husband's—or the viewer's. In that film, as in L'Astrée, all seem to share in its generation. For those who are "outside" the fantasy, however, the sublimation of Céladon into Alexis is entirely unmysterious, prosaic even. Small wonder, therefore, that Phillis and Diane are able to analyze the Alexis situation, pinpointing the subconscious process at work. Diane, in particular, lucidly formulates the curious result of "Alexis's" arrival: "I have since considered that Astrée loved Céladon enormously, and because Alexis looks so much like him, [Astrée] easily was able to feel love for her, since it seemed to her that this figure was still the beloved shepherd; you know that she has always loved only him, and that being her first and only affection, it should not seem strange that when renewed with this girl, it would be very powerful" [4:256]. But if to "outsiders" the process is not so mysterious, the fantastic erotic projection, which seems the collaboration of Céladon and Astrée, predominates in d'Urfé's text, leaving scarcely any room for a more realistic, "scientific" appraisal, such as that of Diane. Harmoniously, the two weave their tale, which ultimately allows for the satisfaction of each within a fiction.

The demand for such a masquerade becomes all the more obvious as Astrée reveals her dream. Here Honoré d'Urfé constructs a totally revealing obsession, one which shows him to have been in full touch with the desires and fears of what we have learned to call the subconscious. Astrée's dream is a transparent revelation of her own fears of Céladon, and of his maleness, of her own sexuality, and it is because of these anxieties that she must receive him as a woman, or banish him as a man:

I dreamed . . . that I entered a thicket heavy with trees and brambles [whose] thorns, after ripping all my clothes (and the darkness of the spot obscuring my vision), pierced my skin at every jab. After struggling for a long time in vain to escape from this miserable predicament, it seemed to me that an individual ["une personne"] whom I could not recognize because of the darkness, approached and said (while averting its face, but extending its hand), that, if I would follow, she would help me out of my predicament. It seemed to me that after thanking her for the aid she had offered, I followed her, still without being able to see, yet [proceeding] with much less difficulty than before; but neither of us could escape from the woods.

Eventually I believe that someone else came between my guide and myself. She grabbed my hand so hard, and I did the same in order not to lose my grip, that the other individual, using all his force ultimately pulled so hard in both ways that the hand I was holding became separated from the arm of the person who had been guiding me; and at the same time it seemed I saw a glimmer of light. This was cause for me to discover, when sadly I tried to see the hand that was left me, that it was really a heart, which continued to pump slowly, until the individual who had made me lose my guide came back holding a large knife; and this figure, however much I tried to stop it, struck a powerful blow to the heart, wounding it so gravely that I found myself covered completely with blood. The horror I then felt caused me to throw it to the ground, but hardly had I done this than I saw the heart transformed into Céladon, and this event caused me such fright that I screamed, as you heard, and at the same time woke up. [4:264-65]

Hearing this narrative, Alexis quickly offers an interpretation of the dream, explaining that the "guide" was none other than herself, and the "person" who wished to separate them was the incarnation of the force which will send her back to the druidesses. The heart, too, is hers, "which will replace Céladon's" [4:265]. But this explanation is designed to shed the most favorable light on the Alexis-Astrée predicament. Alexis does not interpret, but rather paints a picture designed to facilitate her relationship with the shepherdess.

The dream, however, may be seen in another light, for it is so "classic" as to beg for a more psychological probing. The schizophrenic presentation of the lover throughout the episode is duplicated here in Astrée's dream, as two individuals vie for the shepherdess, each nameless, one "une personne" and "she," the other, "someone," but in the masculine form, "quelqu'un," and also

"celui," the masculine form of the demonstrative pronoun.
In this brief passage d'Urfé maintains sexual differentiation, in an otherwise undifferentiated haze, through
close control of grammatical forms, a process which duplicates that of the larger disguise episode which envelops
the dream segment. That the feminine character attempts
to save Astrée from an obscure world filled with brambles, thorns, and trees—all too obvious phallic symbols—and thus from heterosexual adventure, is also
clear, as the figure assumes the almost maternal, sister-
ly role of "guide" and support. This harmony, despite
their futile effort to escape, is interrupted by a
seemingly male presence, who does all in his power to
split apart Astrée and her mentor. When, in this tug of
war, Astrée is left only with her guide's hand, the
process of transformation is complete: the detached hand
of her friend, now a heaving heart, when cast on the
ground by Astrée, is changed into Céladon. Here, the
androgynous myth, so favored in L'Astrée, is intact,
for the hand functions as a double sign, masculine in its
extension, feminine in shape (as well here in its original link to a female-designated character), a phallic
presence which is feminized, hence gentle and protective.
(D'Urfé's dream segment, while composed "as if" in the
mind of Astrée, nonetheless reflects stereotypically
male erotic reveries, which here have been interiorized
by women. His symbolism is traditional in Occidental
literature: power is associated with the man, and protection with the woman.) Finally, in Astrée's dream, the
hand-heart evolves into Céladon, but not without losing
its original association to a female character. This
duplicates the larger episode's gender transformations,
and forms an androgynous Céladon. Here, as in the whole
Astrée-Alexis narrative, the male is tamed, altered by
identification with an almost mythical female spirit: he
is "safe."
    But the masculine figure associated with Céladon in
the dream divides in half. The individual who moves to
separate Astrée from her guide is clearly a male figure,
identified as such by his pronouns. His behavior reflects an effort toward denying Astrée her feminine, at
best androgynous support, in favor of a heterosexual
union, perceived as violent. The knife wielded by this
figure, which severs the androgynously constructed hand/
heart and which causes blood to spurt, may be seen as the
potent phallic symbol, shattering the more gentle, fem-

inized form, and destroying also the protective world
associated with it, a world that is masculine in its
identification with Céladon, but feminized by its initial association with the female guide. The thorns of
the dream's first part, which had pierced Astrée's skin,
are now in extended form a knife, spiller of blood.

In short, this dream, so obvious in its exploitation
of sexual symbolism and in its link to the fairy tales
which seem at moments to share a bond with d'Urfé's
novel, is the reflection in miniature of the whole Alexis-
Astrée episode; it is a fantasy within a fantasy, and
thereby supports the view that the episode is generated,
created by the shepherdess as much as by Céladon, who
ultimately only responds to Astrée's demands. Just as
Astrée's dream conveys in altered form, as dreams do,
her atavistic and intimate fears, so, too, the larger
episode which encompasses it is the sublimated projection
of "safety," into which the male presence is a penetra-
tion, an unwelcome intrusion of danger.

This odd and sensational episode, begun in part 2 and
extending through part 4, is never really "righted."
Céladon-Alexis ultimately reveals his true identity, but
unlike Diane in the Filandre story, Astrée cannot forgive the ruse. Horrified as she recalls the physical
intimacy of her relationship with "Alexis," she can only,
once more, banish Céladon from her sight. The masquerade comes to naught, failing to open onto a field of
genuine self-revelation. Nor is it surprising that this
should be the case, for Céladon, in a nondisguised
state, is threatening to Astrée, not for his ruses, but
for the sexual demands placed on her. From the very
moment that the shepherdess first banishes him—the story
we hear in part 1—Astrée has had a remarkably poor
"case." Her supposed reason for the initial separation
was the shepherd's relationship with Aminthe. Yet, she
herself engineered that subterfuge, and her ready willingness to banish Céladon seems therefore strangely suspect. In part, Astrée is the victim of a suspicious
climate, one in which paranoid attitudes are readily
interiorized. But even this climate of interiorized
suspicion may be explained by the more fundamental one of
fear, and specifically fear of the male. Thus, there can
be no resolution to Astrée and Céladon's dilemma; one
may only anticipate an endless display of wrath alternating with the only ruse—transvestism—which is able to
transcend the fear, allowing as it does for a social-

ly sanctioned and psychologically accepted intimacy.

Hence, it was left to Baro to conclude with an elaborately staged reunion at the "Fontaine de Vérité d'A-
mour." But Baro clearly saw and wished to "correct" the
ambiguous sexuality which d'Urfé exploited in his text.
In Baro's volume, although Céladon is still disguised as
Alexis, he is called Céladon and all the pronouns used
to designate him are masculine. Thus, the ruse exists
for Astrée alone; the reader, conditioned by the male
nouns and pronouns, perceives no ambiguity. And, in
fact, although Astrée is still uninformed, she speaks
lovingly of Céladon, never of Alexis. The shepherd, not
the stand-in, is her conscious and subconscious obsession, thereby obviating the sublimation process, as well
as the homosexual passion which was generated in
d'Urfé's volumes. Baro's text is a morally "correct"
one, and therefore dull, for the key elements of fantasy
romance are removed, denied by the secretary who creates
action to match the elevated ideals of Neoplatonism.
Where d'Urfé, as regards those ideals, subverts, and
some might say perverts, Baro creates a unified fictional
universe governed, and sanitized, by Neoplatonism.

However, as regards the principal disguise episodes in
d'Urfé's four volumes, it becomes increasingly clear
that they are central to the work's structure, for it is
through them that the mechanism of sexual fear and sexual
desire may function. Just as Alexis-Céladon pondered
the strangeness of a dual identity—half desire and half
fear—Astrée, too, and all the "cold" or doubting females, live in this schizophrenic climate, polarized
between their passion and their fear of it. It is therefore not surprising that, like Romeo and Juliet, they are
all the youngest of lovers, living the maddening dilemmas
of adolescents, for whom love problems seem so absolute
as to be beyond resolution. And d'Urfé does not resolve. An untimely death cannot entirely explain such
lack of conclusion. He had, after all, four long parts!
Nor can a desire for reputation and success explain away
his failure to conclude, for with the final banishment of
Céladon, once the Alexis travesty has been played out,
the scenario can only repeat itself. There is little
room for new situations, since Astrée obviously requires
transvestism to fulfill her desire and to reduce her
fear. In short, d'Urfé did not, and probably could not,
conclude, short of the fantastic end Baro imposed on the
text, thereby flagrantly denying its original essence and

flavor. All too often, critics concentrate on Baro's conclusion, as if indeed it made good sense for d'Urfé's book. It does not, for it is these strange disguise episodes, titillating for participants and readers alike, and a genuine textual experiment in generating sexual tension, that lie at the heart of Honoré d'Urfé's massive opus.

Chapter Seven
The Form of *L'Astrée:* Structural and Narrative Considerations

For the contemporary reader of L'Astrée, the single most obvious and significant consideration is the novel's sheer length. Discovering that such mass was typical of the preclassical novel in no way facilitates the reading of these sprawling fictional universes: to the contrary, as increasingly the works of the Scudéry's, La Calprenède, and Gomberville are perused by only a few curious scholars. L'Astrée is commonly read in various highly abridged versions which tend to reduce to one volume the overwhelming mass of the original. Lost, however, in these efforts is the very sense of repetition and inconclusiveness which d'Urfé had created with his lengthy novel. The most frequently read excerpted format, the 10/18 edition, provides only the Astrée-Céladon narrative, a decision which violates to the core the intercalated form that is the essential structural unit of the seventeenth-century French novel, and of L'Astrée in particular. Magendie's 1928 edition includes sections from several principal and secondary narratives, thus making it more representative of the original, but these are generally reduced to two or three page presentations, with the remainder of the story rapidly summarized by the editor. The most recent attempt at abridgment, Maxime Gaume's 1981, one-volume edition, attempts to combine both techniques, offering the story of Céladon and Astrée along with a small sampling of secondary tales.

Of course, all attempts at abridging literary works are ultimately falsifying. But how much more so when all the narratives, save one, are omitted from the "new" format, as in the 10/18 undertaking, or when lengthy, in some cases multivolume tales are reduced to a handful of pages, thereby canceling out the open-ended structure at the base of the original work!

From these abridgments a reader cannot develop a true awareness of the novel's intercalated form; its polyphonic, representative narration; or of the persistent commingling of written and oral forms. Above all, the sense of repetition through, paradoxically, patterned variation is lost, a relief perhaps to the reader who seeks only minimal knowledge of the text, but a clear violation nonetheless of authorial intention. It can be argued that the tale of Céladon and Astrée would be "lost" forever were it not for the 10/18 edition and the new one by Gaume, and this is no doubt true. But the structural composition and unity of L'Astrée may be detected only through the taxing study of the unabridged work. The very length of L'Astrée makes it an encyclopedic compendium, a reflection of the preclassical predilection for including vast numbers of themes, ideas, and structures within the novel format.

The Intercalated Tale

It is only as an abridged title that d'Urfé's massive work has come to be known as L'Astrée. D'Urfé intended a book of multiple narratives, and the full title conveys the work's scope: L'Astrée de Monsieur Honoré d'Urfé ou par plusieurs histoires, et sous personnes de bergers et d'autres sont déduits les divers effets de l'honnête amitié. A multiplicity of tales presented in an interrupted format means that not only the conclusions of principal narratives are thereby deferred, blocked, by an ever-increasing flow of words, but so, too, are those of many of the secondary stories. Some tales do arrive at their conclusion within the confines of one book. Typically, however, a story will be interrupted and then surface again in a subsequent section. D'Urfé not only engenders suspense through this manipulation of the narrative, but also creates a delirious world whereby whole tales and their characters blend one into the other. Distinction and differentiation become close to impossible.

Furthermore, as the intercalated form moves ever inward—with one tale interrupting another, itself a rupture of an earlier one—the intensely word-dependent universe of L'Astrée becomes all the more obvious; for, in the reader's mind, a story "exists" only as long as it is being read. Interrupted, severed, it sustains a temporary death, lost to a new narrative which has supplanted it. Let the reader try to summarize in any detail a story not immediately before his eyes! The labyrinthine structure of intercalated romance creates an entirely verbal universe where stories announce them-

selves as pure language, "existing" only when and as they
are narrated.

The separate story format at this time was hardly
original to Honoré d'Urfé, appearing commonly in the
Spanish pastoral novels which preceded L'Astrée.
Sannazaro's Arcadie and the Diana and its sequels all
utilized this narrative form. The creation of discrete
tales was also a commonplace in French Renaissance fiction, but as Edward Baron Turk has concluded, "d'Urfé
enormously advanced the structural form of the modern
French novel by synthesizing the juxtaposed commentaries
of discrete stories in works like the Heptaméron with
the stories themselves . . ." (1). Thus, d'Urfé, while
complicating the narrative format, could rely on an indi-
genous tradition that was well known to his readership.

But it was principally the Spanish pastoral writers
whom d'Urfé was imitating when he made broad use of discrete stories. As Maxime Gaume has shown in a detailed
section of his work devoted to structural considerations,
d'Urfé carefully followed the format, as established by
the writers of Spanish pastoral fiction. L'Astrée,
for example, shares with these earlier works similar
means for introducing a new story. In the Spanish works,
as in d'Urfé's novel, a story often begins when one
unhappy soul, chanting the misery he has known in love,
and condemning Inconstancy, or Providence, or Fortune, is
overheard by shepherds and shepherdesses hiding behind a
bush or tree. They, in turn, usually invite the forlorn
individual to recount in greater detail his story. Rarely is such an invitation refused! Alternately, strangers
arrive at the center of the pastoral universe (Forez, in
L'Astrée) and confide their tales of woe or attempt to
plead their case before a chosen arbiter. (This technique, employed by the Spanish writers, is common in
L'Astrée, as it allows for the development of the
curious quasi-"legal" judgments.) Again, various shepherds and shepherdesses are sometimes simply invited by
their peers to tell their stories, which they generally
do readily and in great detail (2). This device is
inherently reliable, for, as Turk shows, the universe
constructed on the discrete story base is one of speakers
and listeners. Social life is inherently verbal: people
unite to hear and tell stories (3).

Moreover, in Spanish pastoral fiction and in Honoré
d'Urfé's novel, storytelling occurs in similar surroundings. Tales may erupt in a group, with the various audi-

tors seated in the cool shade of a tree. Often, tales
are told as confidences among a few close friends. In
L'Astrée this is a frequently employed technique for
the stories of the major female figures: Astrée, Diane,
and Phillis divulge and share their tales. Less often, a
messenger arrives at Amasis's court and tells the story
of another character, a story which he himself has
learned only a short time before. Such are the principal
means for beginning a new story, or for continuing one
commenced earlier (4). Once begun, however, the story
surges to the forefront, taking over completely in the
reader's mind and submerging the previous narratives.

In one very significant area, however, Honoré d'Urfé
differs markedly from the majority of his predecessors.
Among the Spanish pastoral writers, only Cervantes had
adopted the technique of the "roman byzantin," whereby a
story is broken off, sometimes quite abruptly, only to be
continued in a later section of the work. Other authors
of pastoral fiction, while interjecting a fair number of
secondary tales into their texts, preferred to terminate
sequentially each one. D'Urfé, like Cervantes, chooses
to fragment his work, interrupting stories sometimes
several times, to create the true intercalated romance
form. Most commonly, the excuse for severing a tale is
that the sun is setting and it is then determined best to
continue the narration the following day. In such cases,
the delay becomes "textual" as well as temporal, for frequently other stories are then spoken and heard, "drowning" the earlier one which resurfaces many pages, books,
or even volumes later. Nor does any one narrative unit—
that is, a tale—necessarily belong to one speaker. Sometimes a tale is told by a wide variety of narrators at
different moments. When a great many pages separate
sections of the story, Honoré d'Urfé carefully recon-
structs in summary form the essential elements of the
narrative, so as not to bewilder his readers, prone to
forget easily! The result is a remarkably tight, well
orchestrated work, far more structurally advanced than
its Spanish predecessors, with d'Urfé readily construct-
ing, interrupting, abandoning, and reconstructing his
multiple narratives (5).

For the reader, nonetheless, there is frequently a
sense of verbal delirium. L'Astrée is convoluted in
its use of intercalated, discrete texts, particularly as
they turn ever inward. Recall, for example, the story of
Alcidon and Daphnide, already intercalated, and yet

itself interrupted by the long narration of Alcyre's
ruse; or of Hylas's narrative, which includes within its
boundaries several other tales. As each one is told its
predecessors, and particularly the encompassing narrative, fades in the reader's mind. Despite d'Urfé's
massive orchestration, events are lost and chronology is
warped, as only the immediate story, the immediate section of a story, seems to exist for us. Perhaps, however, this is the point: L'Astrée is a verbal universe, less a mimetic representation than a work which
persistently calls attention to itself as language. The
"story" is the fundamental narrative unit, and it is the
written transcription of a verbal form. Thus, while
certain intercalated stories remain so, never moving
beyond their fragmented status, others, told separately
for their first segment, ultimately receive their full
status when they are successfully integrated into the
larger textual unit. Galathée's tale, as well as that
of Damon, for example, is initially told in discrete
form, only to be joined to the events and characters of
the larger—but always verbal—universe that is L'Astrée. Her story links up with that of Céladon and
Astrée, creating a powerfully well orchestrated tale.
It is this merger of stories, this joining of language to
language, which forms the structural base of d'Urfé's
opus.

Such writing produces a sense of open-endedness,
common in the novels of the time, although it is not
clear whether this reflects authorial failure or intent.
It may well be that only the artificially imposed ending
of a Baro could engender termination, a choice d'Urfé
(and his peers) could not themselves make. In any case,
structurally speaking, fragmentation is the rule, and an
inevitable sense of discontinuity prevails.

From the perspective of theme, however, this is not
the case. While each discrete narrative as it is being
read seems an entity unto itself, in many instances the
secondary tales are clear reflections of the principal
ones. Not only are the fundamentals duplicated—love,
treachery, faithlessness or the fear of it—but so, too,
are the plot elements which ultimately should serve to
create a sense of distinction and differentiation. In
one striking example of a secondary narrative patterned
after the primary one of Céladon and Astrée, Daphnide
comes to believe that Alcidon really loves Clarinte,
although it was Daphnide herself who created the ruse of

the Alcidon-Clarinte romance. Her doubt mirrors perfectly that of Astrée who, having invented the Céladon-
Aminthe subterfuge, becomes genuinely suspicious of the
situation which she had formed. Moreover, in the same
secondary tale, Alcidon comes to believe, on a specious
rumor, that Daphnide had been unfaithful to him, just as
Astrée, too, had doubted Céladon's fidelity, despite
(in both instances) much proof to the contrary.

There are differences, of course, between the two
stories. While the basic pattern of self-engendered
suspicion and of rumor based doubt is unchanged, it is
Astrée's role that is duplicated in the behavior of both
Daphnide and Alcidon. This shift is significant:
Alcidon, the male of one story, comes to doubt in the
same fashion as Astrée, the female of the other. In
this instance, however, Alcidon merely reverses the
pattern of the primary narrative, reverses Céladon's
situation. The names alone tell all, for the first two
syllables of each man's name are reversed, while the last
is identical. Such anagrammatic games are common in
L'Astrée, and rarely occur gratuitously, reflecting a
close if not identical situation. Here, a syllabic reversal conveys a mirror-image pattern. But, in assuming
Astrée's posture of doubt, while having his identity
merged to Céladon's through their maleness and their
alike names, Alcidon becomes a perfectly androgynous
figure, and therefore the metonymic representation of the
work's primary tale.

In short, despite the mass and length of Honoré
d'Urfé's novel, there is a curious similarity to much of
the work. Are we therefore to conclude that the man
lacked imagination and was simply unable to create a
greater variety of situations and themes? Such a conclusion, tempting perhaps for those wearied by the monotony
of reading through L'Astrée, seems premature. The
name patterning alone, by which d'Urfé almost codifies
his story duplication, suggests a deliberate attempt at
the illusion of variation within a fundamentally repeti-
tious, even obsessive framework, rather than an insuffi-
ciently varied approach to writing. The result is a
highly static work.

Narration/Narrator

The illusion of variety in what is a monotonous uni-

verse of love gone awry is sustained not only through
similarity of plot situation, but also through narrative
construction. D'Urfé's novel is, above all else, a
storyteller's universe, where speakers and auditors come
together to form the book that is L'Astrée. Diegesis
is the dominant form, as description tends to be both
sparse and brief. But who is the narrator? At times,
one hears the so-called "authorial" voice, or more accurately, a narrative presence that in the reader's mind is
most closely allied with the author—an illusion, perhaps, but a traditionally powerful one. Most frequently,
however, the stories of L'Astrée are told by the
book's characters themselves, that is, by representative
narrators who, speaking alternately, appear to create a
polyphonic world, whereby each may be in turn speaker and
auditor.

The omniscience of the "authorial" narrator is, moreover, duplicated by the representative narrators (that
is, the characters), for whom there are no secrets, no
unknown facts. Verisimilitude is not an issue here. In
part, the ability of each narrator to construct, or
rather, to reconstruct not only his or her tale, but that
of someone else as well, is the result of a situational
nightmare in which there are no secrets or private
knowledge. Forez, we have seen, is an inferno of public
awareness, and consequently each and all are privy to
every bit of information, even that deemed the most
private and intimate. Moreover, knowledge here inevitably implies telling, "spilling the beans"; stories are
created out of this impulse for public revelation.

But there is more to the narrative structure of L'Astrée than this publication of all events, both major
and minor. In d'Urfé's novel, the intercalated form,
whereby a story is often split, fragmented, its linearity
broken, creates the need for another or other narrators
who ultimately finish what was so abruptly curtailed.
Furthermore, even when a story is told in unbroken linearity, it may sustain more than one representative narrator. At such times, narrative threads are simply picked
up by a listener, who then becomes a coauthor of the
tale. The variations on such practice of polyphonic
narration are many. In one instance, Diane and Astrée
relate in great detail the story of Olimpe's pregnancy,
reputedly a "secret," known to but a few. Yet, both
girls readily narrate the tale of her downfall, their
supposedly separate voices muted into one well orchestra-

ted account. In another instance, both Daphnide and
Alcidon recount their story, each contributing significantly to its formulation. Sometimes a tangential figure
will tell a tale, as when it is left to Merindor to conclude the story of Sigismonde, Dorinde, and Gondebaud.
The new narrator is always, in such instances, as compe-
tent in storytelling as were the intimate participants of
the tale.

Increasingly apparent from this shifting of narrative
voice is not merely the degree to which everything is
common knowledge in Forez, but also, from a structural
viewpoint, how little the use of polyphonic narration
alters the content of what is being told. The inter-
changeability of narrative voice, the fact that shifts
may and do occur in midstream, or that one character may
finish a tale elaborately begun by another, with no sense
of loss on the reader's part, signifies that in L'Astrée the narrator is far less important than the narration. In fact, recognition of narrative voice is often
impossible: a tale winds on for so long without reference to the speaker that the reader can no longer recall
who is narrating. Such a "loss" occurs even for those
tales related by one speaker, but is all the more
prominent when a shift occurs in narrative voice, or when
a tale is fragmented, its parts dispersed in different
books or volumes. This loss of speaker identity, however, has absolutely no bearing at all on the effect of
the narrative. Rather, the narration of L'Astrée
occurs in almost a speakerless void where differentiation
is only illusory. Even in those narratives where a
judgment is to be pronounced, and where distinction would
seem to be essential as each "defendant" testifies on his
or her behalf, there is a sense of a vacuum, a sense that
the ongoing speech emanates less from a partisan than a
"coauthor," one whose voice is strikingly like the opponent's! Of course, in these cases a difference in
perspective is necessary: Célidée stresses subjugation
to her male suitors, while they highlight what they
perceive as gross injustices to their own persons. Such
a difference in opinion, however, in no way colors the
speech act itself, which remains remarkably indistinct.
Moreover, even in those instances of partisan dispute, it
is not so much that facts are contested by opposing
defendants, but rather that different ones are continually offered. Debates in L'Astrée offer less a multiple
perspective on a same predicament than new and integral

parts of a whole story. Each speaker, then, contributes
to the tale's unfolding.
     In short, L'Astrée is a solo, with one voice repeat-
ing one obsessive theme of love, inconstancy, and jealousy. It matters not who is speaking, or that verisimilitude is so lacking that a Ligdamon, for one, can tell
word for word what was said in a conversation that took
place while he was totally unconscious! There is only
one true narrative voice in L'Astrée, despite the
illusion of a polyphonic chant, just as ultimately there
is only one story, told again and again, and just as
there are characters whose names virtually duplicate themselves and to whom remarkably similar events occur.
     L'Astrée is a trap. Massively long, it promises
therefore great variety, and offers instead repetition,
variations on a theme which vary little. The lack of
distinction among the characters, their vaguely deline-
ated identities, become necessities in a fictional
universe where the sharply defined "self" has no place.
Here, an indistinguishable voice, an undifferentiated
narrator tells only one story of the folly of loving,
known, predictably, to all in Forez, and, by extension,
to the whole human race.

Judgments, Letters, Poems, and Songs

     Within the narrative of L'Astrée, authorial or rep-
resentative, exists an alternate text, entirely separate
in form, yet integral in theme to the larger structure
which encompasses it. More precisely, there are several
other texts, incorporating a remarkably diversified variety of oral and written forms of communication. Letters,
poems, songs, debates, and judgments, all coexist with
each other and with the basic diegesis, testimony to
d'Urfé's effort to include the structures of occidental
literary tradition along with the themes.
     JUDGMENTS. The debates and judgments are in one way
most closely connected to the fundamental narrative, that
is, to the stories per se. Many of the tales revolve
precisely around a judgment: two or more characters come
to plead their case in Forez, before an arbiter, commonly
Adamas or one of the nymphs, sometimes a principal shepherd or shepherdess. Their plea becomes their story,
which they recount to the judges and assembled auditors,
who gather almost as a jury. At the conclusion, a deci-

sion in favor of one party or the other is pronounced by
the judge. All these pleas and judgments maintain a
wholly narrative role, as opposed to other debates in
L'Astrée—those between Hylas and Silvandre, Adamas
and Hylas, or Céladon and Hylas—which are philosophical
digressions interrupting the flow of the diegesis. Thus,
Tircis and Laonice plead their case, and reveal their
story, each a defendant supporting mutually exclusive
positions: Tircis seeks to be faithful to the memory of
Cléon, now dead, and Laonice demands that he free himself of such bonds in order to love her. Célidée's
plea-narration reveals a demand for her liberty, while
Thamire and Calidon separately attempt to convince that
each is worthy of her hand. And Doris, distressed and
weary from the machinations of Palémon and Adraste,
recounts her sorry tale in pleading for her freedom from
both men, while they defend the opposite point of view.
　The effect of such debating and pleading is double.
On the one hand, these judgment-oriented accounts interrupt and therefore retard the outcome of previously established narratives. On the other, they serve to introduce
a new narrative unit. Yet, while novelty is inherently
suggested, the new units tend to repeat the fundamental
themes of the diegesis (itself parcelized and fragmented
into separate story components, which also seemed to
promise novelty and which produce, instead, similarity,
as each recounts its tale of passion gone haywire). The
quasi-legal, rhetorically based judgments offer the
appearance of distinction, while nonetheless reiterating
the same essential tale. Here, as elsewhere, the "trio"
format—real or imagined—surfaces; here, too, the woman
sees herself as prey to aggressive male tendencies. And
when that format is not an issue—as in the Tircis-
Laonice drama—the story still mirrors aspects found in
other significant episodes. Tircis's fidelity to
Cléon's memory reflects that of Diane to Filandre; and
Laonice's angry frustration in not successfully "snaring"
Tircis recalls Galathée's wrath when Céladon insisted
on total fidelity to Astrée. Both Laonice and
Galathée, in their separate tales, convey a sense of
frustration due to obstacle, of blocked passion, that is
the mark of extreme desire, as well as that of L'Astrée. In short, despite their formal separation from
the narrative flow, and their semijuridical nature, the
principal judgment episodes tend to pattern themselves
after the work's other narratives. They are the twins of

the stories recounted in the fundamental diegesis, themselves the illusion of oral testimony through the medium
of writing. Thus, the court-judgment episodes serve to
extend both thematically and structurally the essential
L'Astrée: endless verbal exchange of love matters.
The episodes are a capsulized form, a miniature, of the
superstructure (6).
    LETTERS. Yet more dramatically than the judgments and
pronouncements, letters in L'Astrée appear to rupture
the smooth surface, the continuity of the narration.
They stand out dramatically, for they are set off typo-
graphically by blank white spaces from the regular narrative; they receive a heading, typically "Letter from A to
B"; and they are always presented in italics (7). Moreover, they reverse the usual pattern for L'Astrée:
whereas the diegesis offers the illusion of oral discourse through a written format, the letters often appear
as the reverse: verbal renditions (but word for word!)
of texts that once were written down. (Of course, the
illusion is compounded by the fact that L'Astrée, a
novel, remains always a printed text, and therefore recon-
verts the oral status of letter-telling to its original
written form.) Verisimilitude is once more laid to rest,
as letters are recounted in a fashion utterly faithful to
their original written form, or so we are led to believe.
It is not unusual to "hear" a character divulge orally
an entire correspondence verbatim, as Léonide does for
her exchange with Lindamor!
    The letters, too, however, are intimately connected to
the larger narrative of which they are an integral part.
The missives, while less overtly related to the normal
narrative flow than are the judgment episodes which form
whole stories, nonetheless are charged with advancing the
plot and with reflecting the characters' predicaments.
The use of letters was hardly an innovation in the novel
at the time Honoré d'Urfé composed L'Astrée. The
tradition goes back to antiquity and to the Greek
romances. More immediately, the Renaissance pastorals
had utilized letters as a supplement to the fundamental
narrative. In the Spanish pastoral novels, letters
appear, but their appearance is rather limited:
Montemayor's Diana has nine, and Cervantes's Galatea,
ten. Thus, while d'Urfé did not innovate in choosing to
employ the letter format, he was original in his decision
to extend significantly their role. Each part of L'Astrée contains twelve or more letters—part 1 alone

contains thirty-eight—and their frequency in the text
shifts their status from narrative ornament to supple-
mental diegesis. And the letters do fulfill, again both
thematically and formally, the demands imposed on them by
the larger, encompassing unit.

Maxime Gaume has summarized well the multiple functions of letters in the universe of L'Astrée. Sometimes they engender joy, sometimes anxiety or depression,
for frequently letters are charged to express feelings
that the characters may not wish or be able to express in
direct communication. They may be cause for great upset
if they fall into the hands of a rival in love. When
letters are forged, they become a powerful means of
deception. In short, as an activator, the letter becomes
an integral part of a given narrative, allowing for the
expression of feelings and, concomitantly, for the
advancement of the plot (8). Gaume's analysis that the
letters are distinct from the narrative, yet part of it,
is precise: formally distinct, they nonetheless join the
encompassing narrative structure, doubling and reinforcing it, a metonymic unit.

Taken together, a group of letters may be a capsulized
miniature, an essential abstraction of an entire relationship, hence, of an entire narrative. As Gaume demonstrates, the correspondence between Céladon and Astrée
recounts their developing passion, thereby joining and
doubling the principal narration as elaborated by Astrée,
which also described their nascent love for one another.
When, however, the letters are intercepted by Alcippe,
and when one is forged by Sémire, the purpose of the correspondence is less to recount than to open onto new narrative possibilities, beyond the letter. And when, following Sémire's betrayal, and Céladon's suicidal plunge
into the Lignon, the hero finds himself a virtual prisoner in Galathée's palace, the correspondence he has preserved serves to intensify the princess's passion, thereby increasing and extending narrative possibilities (9).

The letters of L'Astrée thus appear to serve a
double purpose: a summary reflection of previous narrative which becomes a metonymic commentary on that narrative, and, second, a means to create further incidents,
that is, new narrative. Within the text L'Astrée,
within the parameters of the basic diegetic structure,
there exists an almost self-contained epistolary novel,
simultaneously a reflection and generator of the traditional narrative unit.

POEMS AND SONGS. Just as the letter, with its distinctive presentation and format, is one step more removed from the fundamental diegesis than is the "plaidoyer," so, too, the poem-song indicates yet a further separation. While the judgment episodes and letters are "interrupters" in the narrative, they at least are still prose, and thus continue smoothly the word flow of the text. The shift to verse format, however, is a far more radical departure, implying a dramatic break in continuity for the reader, one, moreover, that will disappear shortly after L'Astrée: Polexandre, for example, contains no islets of verse. But L'Astrée is not yet that "new" form, and verse occupies a prominent place in its composition. Nor is this is a surprising fact: ostensibly a pastoral romance, d'Urfé's novel had to utilize verse if it was to remain faithful to the pastoral conventions.

This is surely one reason why so many sonnets, madrigals, and "chansons" appear in L'Astrée. Yet another reason is that d'Urfé saw himself as a poet, he wrote a great deal of verse, and was himself a part of a larger Renaissance culture in which poetry was enormously significant as a literary genre. As it turns out, a considerable number of the poems which appear in L'Astrée were composed before the novel itself. In fact, Maxime Gaume has discovered that among those d'Urfé poems which were published in poetry collections at the beginning of the seventeenth century, only twelve do not appear in L'Astrée (10)! This remarkable fact, however, should lead not to the conclusion of Boileau in the Discours préliminaire to Les Héros du roman, that the whole of L'Astrée was a mere excuse for highlighting d'Urfé's poetic reputation (one, incidentally, that Boileau finds undeserved), but rather to the recognition that structurally at least the poems and songs of L'Astrée are truly independent entities, separately publishable texts, which sharply rupture and intrude on the diegetic prose norm.

The truth is that without the verse which d'Urfé sprinkles so liberally throughout his text, the lyrical premise at the base of all pastoral literature would be sorely in question; for despite the rustic setting, despite the tendency toward solitary introspection and prolific sighing, L'Astrée persistently refuses a steadfast place in pastoral fiction. Along with the country decor and the other explicit signs of "la bergerie," the lyrical verse format is itself the mark of pastoral romance. Without it, the book would be "other," and no doubt Gomberville recognized this, for his adventure-laden work is a sharp departure from that form: removed from the traditional country setting it also refuses to integrate verse into its narration. Polexandre has quit the pastoral world; L'Astrée, while surpassing it, nonetheless integrates poetry into a prose world, as d'Urfé seeks to incorporate a veritable conglomeration of occidental literary forms.

The verse itself is unremarkable, highly conventional in its choice of themes. Not surprisingly, the poems and songs reflect and extend precisely the lyrical, pastoral aspects of the work, and beyond that, of Renaissance expression. The poems of L'Astrée offer the traditional motifs of desire and obstacle, of love's heartaches and joys, of the shepherdess's great beauty, of inconstancy, of eyes that lure and betray. Such expression both serves to duplicate and thereby reinforce the sense of love's totality which is expressed countless times in prose throughout the novel, and to reflect and integrate Western literary themes, particularly those of the Renaissance, themselves reflections of intellectual currents born in antiquity. The poems and songs become an alternate means for d'Urfé to vary his structure, for him to signal his desire to remain within the pastoral format, while at the same time allowing for the repetition—alas, once more—of the network of themes which dominates in the prose sections of the book.

Maxime Gaume has attempted to trace the precise origins of many of L'Astrée's poems, and he adequately conveys the debt that d'Urfé owed to Renaissance French poets, as well as to those of Italy. Indeed, some of the similarities which Gaume demonstrates exist between d'Urfé's verse and that of Desportes or Tasso almost suggest plagiarism! But Gaume prefers to insist on a communal spirit shared by many sixteenth- and early seventeenth-century poets in order to explain the parallels between d'Urfé's art and that of the era's other major poets. The Petrarchan tradition strongly marked an entire literary generation, and it is this inheritance which is at the base of the poetry of L'Astrée (11).

Gaume's effort is a worthy one in that he tries to situate d'Urfé's verse within a larger cultural climate; but beyond establishing a basic core of similarities such an attempt may not be really necessary for understanding the role poetry plays in L'Astrée. By offering to his readers islets of verse, d'Urfé clearly establishes a

pastoral foundation for his novel; moreover, poetry provides yet another means for lodging his principal themes
of love and its joys and sorrows within a varied structural framework. The poetry, more even than the book's many
letters, signals the lyric side of L'Astrée—a musical
accompaniment to the plaintive prose wailing which occurs
throughout the work. That such melancholy is only one
aspect of L'Astrée—for there is also Hylas's unbridled freedom, Childéric's unchecked lust, Galathée's
endless plotting, and Céladon's voyeurism—does nothing
to diminish the significance of the verse format. Poetry
appears in L'Astrée as a double of the lyrical prose
passages, or perhaps the reverse is more accurate: the
sections devoted to contemplation and introspection, to
expressing keenly felt sentiments in love matters, are
the prose transcriptions of the earlier lyrical, poetic
forms in Western literature.   L'Astrée offers the
transformation of poetry into prose (while still maintaining the former), and in so doing presents the genesis of
the French novel.

Conclusion

In short, no "shifter," no interrupter in d'Urfé's
text truly ruptures the continuum of thought. The smooth
flow of prose, of the fundamental diegetic structure, is
broken, of course, to some degree by harangues and judgments, more so by letters, and yet more by verse. But
such shifting is essentially an illusion of rupture and
of change, for while the narrative itself is temporarily
displaced, the fundamental themes are not: they are, in
fact, only reinforced by a continued focus on the problems of love.   Just as d'Urfé created the illusion of
polyphonism, and just as he used the intercalated romance
form to achieve the appearance of variety, all in a
universe given over precisely to the sameness of the
human predicament, so, too, does the author of L'Astrée, through rhetorically based judgments, through letters, and through verse, convey a variety of forms which
nonetheless obsessively repeat the same concepts found in
the fundamental narrative.   In L'Astrée, there is no
variety, no movement, no progression: ultimately, there
is only one voice telling its one tale, over and over
again.

Chapter Eight
Conclusion

Despite a critical examination of the type offered here, it is all too clear that for most readers, the novel as it was practiced by Mlle de Scudéry, by La Calprenède, or by d'Urfé remains a strange phenomenon. The alienation is not temporal, for, as noted earlier, it does not exist for Mme de Lafayette's works. Rather, the problem is essentially a physical one: in La Princesse de Clèves, for example, the form is so altered, in its newfound concision, as to seem the flagrant denial of the multivolume works common in the early decades of the seventeenth century. No exegesis will change the fact that the massive novels which d'Urfé and his peers produced are unfamiliar to, and perhaps even uncomfortable for, contemporary sensibilities.

When nineteenth-century French novelists attempted to capture nothing less than the "world" in their writing, they did so through discrete volumes, which, taken together, could legitimately constitute a series, but which were also integral, independent units unto themselves. Balzac's La Comédie Humaine and, to a lesser degree, Zola's Les Rougon-Macquart are collective titles which tie together a loosely linked group of novels, each of which may be, and in fact is, read separately.

That contemporary readers do not respond to L'Astrée in the same way as they do to La Princesse de Clèves, reflects primarily a lost reading habit: the ability to focus on a large mass of material rarely presented in linear fashion. Modern novels are considered long if they reach four hundred pages in one volume! On the visual plane, however, matters are somewhat different. Television is adept at "stringing along" its viewers, interrupting and severing tales, continuing them, interjecting new ones alongside the old. In this relatively new medium we concentrate well enough to follow episode after episode in numerous daytime, and, now, evening series. But it is all too clear that this experience will not be duplicated for the novel. As it developed in the West, and despite some exceptions (in

France, for example, during the period between World Wars
I and II), the novel has regularly eliminated the scope,
the mass that mark works such as L'Astrée, which, even
though it was initially read part by part, offered for
each such "tome" a vast and wordy universe.

For all great literary works—and L'Astrée is unquestionably one—there are strong elements within them
that please and interest different generations (or even
groups within the same generation) of readers. The "précieuses" focused on the abstract, intellectual passages
of d'Urfé's novel, on the words of Adamas and Silvandre,
and found much to their liking. These are precisely the
sections which tire most contemporary readers of L'Astrée, who prefer (as no doubt did many readers in
d'Urfé's time), the "zero degree" eroticism, so deftly
created and manipulated. Equally intriguing to modern
scholarship are the diverse techniques employed by
Honoré d'Urfé to create his narrative structure.
Rhetorically, there are whole sections—harangues,
debates, judgments—which may be studied for their ties
to classical forms, and for their role in an essentially
diegetic composition. Moreover, the question of narrative perspective, of who says what, where, how, and why,
should continue to interest contemporary readers: storytelling per se still preoccupies our writers—Borges, for
one, and cinematographers—Buñuel, for another (1).

There are perhaps scholars who will question whether
such fields of inquiry are appropriate, believing that
these perspectives are strictly conjectural for a work
written so long ago, and, they may believe, for vastly
different reasons. For these critics, an approach which
situates L'Astrée in post-Renaissance culture and
literature, or one that links it to biographical information on d'Urfé and his family, is more pure. But any
literary work may only be studied with pleasure if it is
seen as offering a link to the preoccupations and interests of the culture which chooses to embrace it. As we
read literature, we perhaps rewrite it, but short of that
experience there is no vitality to the act. L'Astrée,
given a chance, its mass and length transcended, provides
an occasion for such radical communion.

Notes and References

Chapter One

1. Gérard Genette, "Le Serpent dans la Bergerie," in L'Astrée (Paris, 1964), p. 8.

2. The most up-to-date and thorough study of d'Urfé's intellectual background is Gaume's Les Inspirations et les sources de l'oeuvre d'Honoré d'Urfé (Saint-Etienne, 1977). This thesis, which incorporates and transcends previously published material, proved invaluable for my own presentation of d'Urfé's life. The section of Gaume's work which concentrates on life at La Bastie and the intellectual climate of Renaissance Forez appears in pp. 18-40.

3. Ibid., pp. 40-41, 42-53.

4. Ibid., pp. 55-101.

5. Ibid., p. 114. See pp. 102-43 for a discussion of d'Urfé's exposure to, and use of, historical texts.

6. Ibid., p. 59.

7. For a brief but complete analysis of the role played by the d'Urfé family in the League, see Sister Mary Catherine McMahon, Aesthetics and Art in the "Astrée" of Honoré d'Urfé (New York, 1969), pp. 20-21. A more detailed analysis may be found in O.-C. Reure, La Vie et les oeuvres de Honoré d'Urfé (Paris, 1910), pp. 34-55.

8. Both Gaume and Reure in their respective studies offer complete descriptions of the composition of the Epistres Morales. Our discussion of this work in the present volume is brief, for it is not widely read or available. The Epistres Morales do offer, however, a point of departure for understanding certain metaphysical concepts expressed throughout L'Astrée.

9. Gaume, Les Inspirations, pp. 156-62.

10. For Reure, La Savoysiade is such an inferior work that he chooses to devote only a couple of pages to its description. Gaume, on the other hand, devotes pp. 231-73 of his study to detailing the genesis of this poem and its literary debts to other epic works.

11. Reure, Honoré d'Urfé, pp. 90-97, 132, 184-86, 187-203; McMahon, Aesthetics, pp. 24-25.

12. Reure, Honoré d'Urfé, p. 171; McMahon, Aesthetics, p. 25. On more than one occasion, Reure refuses to qualify the separation between Honoré d'Urfé and Diane de Châteaumorand as anything but amiable. In fact, he is even reluctant to describe the time they spent apart as a "separation."

Controversy continues to surround the authorship of the fourth part of L'Astrée. Most scholars now believe that it is the work of d'Urfé, refined slightly perhaps by Balthazar Baro. In terms of structure, style, and theme, the fourth part remains faithful to the first three, while the fifth marks an obvious shift.

Regarding the fifth part, there is yet another controversy. While it has traditionally been believed that Baro completed d'Urfé's work, recently Bernard Yon has made a convincing case for attributing the "real" conclusion to Gomberville, a task occasioned by d'Urfé attempting to switch publishers, but then dying before the completion of his novel. The fascinating account of these maneuvers may be read in Yon's introduction to "L'Astrée"--VIème partie: La Suite de Gomberville (Saint-Etienne, 1976).

I have not attempted here to resolve who wrote the "real" sequel, since the question is incidental to a study of Honoré d'Urfé. For the purposes of the present work, I consider the first four parts as those of d'Urfé. A handful of references are made to Baro's conclusion, since traditionally it is considered part of the published whole that is L'Astrée.

13. See Reure, Honoré d'Urfé, pp. 347-51, for a description of the Valteline episode.

14. See Gaume, Les Inspirations, pp. 556-82.

Chapter Two

1. Northrop Frye, The Anatomy of Criticism (Princeton: Princeton University Press, 1957), p. 304.

2. Gaume, Les Inspirations, pp. 507-10.

3. Ibid., pp. 510-14.

4. Jacques Ehrmann, Un Paradis désespéré: l'amour et l'illusion dans "L'Astrée" (New Haven, 1963), p. 12.

5. Gaume, Les Inspirations, pp. 546-47.

6. Related background information on traditional

pastoral plots, themes, and forms may be found in ibid., pp. 584-616.

7. Honoré d'Urfé, L'Astrée, ed. Hugues Vaganay (Geneva, 1966), 1:6-7; hereafter cited in the text. In my translations of d'Urfé's text I have attempted to render the English prose as "modern" as possible, without violating the sense of the original passages.

8. Aside from Jacques Ehrmann, whose study is marked by references to the river's importance, various critics have portrayed the Lignon as highly significant to the unfolding of the various dramas in L'Astrée. See M. Gerhardt, "Un Personnage principal de L'Astrée: Le Lignon," pp. 47-56, and Maurice Debesse, "Le Pays de L'Astrée," pp. 31-45, both in Colloque commémoratif du quatrième centenaire de la naissance d'Honoré d'Urfé (Montbrison, 1970).

9. Gaume, Les Inspirations, p. 179.

10. Ehrmann, Un Paradis désespéré, pp. 88-90.

11. Gaume, Les Inspirations, pp. 116-32.

Chapter Three

1. Edward Baron Turk, Baroque Fiction-Making: A Study of Gomberville's "Polexandre" (Chapel Hill, 1978), p. 46.

2. Northrop Frye, The Secular Scripture: A Study of the Structure of Romance (Cambridge, Mass.: Harvard University Press, 1976), p. 54.

3. Turk reaches a similar conclusion regarding Polexandre: "The anagram-like configurations suggested by the syllabic makeup of the proper names must be appreciated as a further constitutive element in the larger scheme of the novel. As such, it can be seen to reflect the two most basic features of its form: the dispersal of discrete syllables in protean contexts reinforces the sense of motility and instability, whereas the very recurrence of the same syllables forming networks of concatenated segments reinforces the ultimate sense of interrelatedness and fused integrity" (p. 51).

Chapter Four

1. Frye, The Secular Scripture, p. 24.

2. Gaume, Les Inspirations, p. 432.

3. Ibid., pp. 438-50.

4. Ibid., pp. 441-47.

5. Ibid., p. 472.

Chapter Five

1. Clifton Cherpack, "Form and Ideas in L'Astrée," Studies in Philology 69 (July 1972):333.
Cherpack forthrightly, and correctly, denies the concept
of harmony in L'Astrée, and he examines d'Urfé's
novel from the basic premise of precisely such a "lack."
2. Ibid., pp. 332-33.
3. Ehrmann, Un Paradis désespéré, p. 58. See
also Jean Charron, "Le Thème de la 'Métamorphose' dans
L'Astrée," Dix-septième siècle, no. 101 (1973),
pp. 3-13.
4. Ehrmann, Un Paradis désespéré, p. 91.
5. Ibid., p. 44.
6. Jean Rousset, Le Mythe de Don Juan (Paris:
Armand Colin, 1978), pp. 120-29.
7. Hylas's third table: "Never setting limits to
his desire, / May he search for pleasure everywhere, /
Perpetually loving anew, / Indeed, may he cease loving
her, / Except insofar as loved by her, / For his own
purposes will he esteem her."
Hylas's eighth table: "Warmed only by a slow burn-
ing flame, / May he never be burned, / Nor may he ever
sigh and languish / Between life and death: / And may he
always be able to say / What he wants, and what he
doesn't."
Hylas's twelfth table: "May he never think / That
such love is eternal: / Whoever advises him otherwise /
Let him be deemed an enemy, / For just listening to him /
Is a crime of 'lèse-majesté.'"

Chapter Six

1. Turk, Baroque Fiction-Making, p. 129.
2. Gaume, Les Inspirations, p. 613.
3. Ibid.
4. Ehrmann, Un Paradis désespéré, pp. 80-81,
convincingly formulates this double, hetero/homosexual
perspective.
5. Ibid., pp. 55-56.

Chapter Seven

1. Turk, Baroque Fiction-Making, p. 62.

2. Gaume, Les Inspirations, pp. 599-600.

3. Turk, Baroque Fiction-Making, p. 33.

4. Gaume, Les Inspirations, p. 600.

5. Ibid., pp. 600-601.

6. For a detailed discussion of the judicial format in L'Astrée, see Daniel Chouinard, "L'Astrée et la rhétorique: L'adaptation romanesque du genre judiciaire," Papers on French Seventeenth Century Literature 10, no. 2 (1978):41-56.

7. Turk, Baroque Fiction-Making, pp. 96-97, makes similar remarks regarding the letter format in Polexandre. He then proceeds to show how Gomberville altered the typically clumsy letter format by omitting terms such as "Lettre" or "Billet" from the heading, thereby creating "a strong integration of the letter with the rest of the narrative" (p. 97).

8. Gaume, Les Inspirations, p. 604.

9. Ibid., pp. 604-5.

10. Ibid., p. 619.

11. See ibid., pp. 621-48, for a thorough comparison of d'Urfé's poetry to European-wide Renaissance traditions.

Chapter Eight

1. Myriam Yvonne Jehenson, in The Golden World of the Pastoral (Ravenna, Italy, 1981), briefly studies the question of narrative perspective in L'Astrée, showing that there are major discrepancies in the narrated versions of events by diverse characters. The examples she provides on page 148 of her book are all sound, and serve to show the importance of perspective in the fundamental narrative format of the story (as opposed to the debate format, intent on accumulating new information via the diverse participants' discourses). Her brief remarks should be incorporated into a larger study of this question.

Selected Bibliography

PRIMARY SOURCES

1. Original editions
La Sylvanire, ou la Mort-vive. Paris: Robert Fouet,
   1627. The "privilège du roi" accorded Fouet is from
   12 April 1625.

2. Recent editions
L'Astrée. Edited by Hugues Vaganay, 5 vols. 1925.
   Reprint. Geneva: Slatkine Reprints, 1966.
Les Epistres Morales. Geneva: Slatkine, 1973.
Le Sireine. Edited by J.-C. Marcos. Salamanca:
   Editions universitaires, 1979.
La Triomphante Entrée de Très illustre Dame Magdeleine
   de la Rochefoucauld. Edited by Maxime Gaume. Saint-
   Etienne: CITAC (Presses de l'Université de Saint-
   Etienne), 1976.

3. Manuscripts
La Savoysiade. MS 2959, Bibliothèque de l'Arsenal,
   Paris. Considered definitive edition.

4. Excerpted editions of L'Astrée
Gaume, Maxime. L'Astrée. Saint-Etienne: Le Hénaff,
   1981. Paperback. The most recent excerpted edition.
   Includes material from both primary and secondary
   tales. Brief introductory and bibliographical material; helpful notes.
Genette, Gérard. Honoré d'Urfé: "L'Astrée."
   Paris: Union générale d'éditions, 1964. Collection 10/18. Preceded by "Le Serpent dans la
   Bergerie." Most commonly read abridged edition,
   offering Astrée-Céladon tale. Provocative introduction.
Magendie, Maurice. "L'Astrée." Analyse et Extraits.
   Paris: Perrin, 1928. Includes several principal and
   secondary tales in highly abridged format.

SECONDARY SOURCES

Bochet, Henri. "L'Astrée": ses origines, son influence dans la formation de la littérature classique.
1923. Reprint. Geneva: Slatkine Reprints, 1967. A
general presentation of L'Astrée, focusing on Platonism, sources, and style.

Bonnet, Jacques. La symbolique de "L'Astrée."
Saint-Etienne: Le Hénaff, 1981. A new and
provocative study, concentrating on symbolic aspects
of L'Astrée, particularly temporal and spatial
representation, numbers, geometrical configurations,
and mythological figures.

Calì, Andrea, and Ferrandes, Carmela. "L'Infrazione al
Codice: Il 'déguisement' nell' 'Astrée' di Honoré
d'Urfé." In Il Romanzo al tiempo de Luigi XIII.
Bari: Adriatica; Paris: Nizet, 1976, pp. 13-38.
Studies the principal disguise episodes of the Astrée-
Céladon story in light of structural and linguistic
concepts.

Carroll, M. G. "L'Astrée or Virtue Corrupted."
Trivium 8 (May 1973):27-36. Suggests that Forez is
a "fallen world," failing to attain the spiritualism
of the courtly codes.

Charron, Jean. "Le Thème de la 'Métamorphose' dans
L'Astrée." Dix-septième siècle, no. 101
(1973), pp. 3-13. A well presented introduction to
the "Alexis" episode.

Cherpack, Clifton. "Form and Ideas in L'Astrée."
Studies in Philology 69 (July 1972):320-33. An
excellent article, conveying the fragmented instability of L'Astrée.

Chouinard, Daniel. "L'Astrée et la rhétorique:
l'adaptation romanesque du genre judiciaire." Papers
on French Seventeenth Century Literature 10, no. 2
(1978):41-56. Inspired by Laugaa's suggestions, a
technical but worthy discussion of d'Urfé's use of
the judicial format within the fundamental narrative
unit.

Colloque commémoratif du quatrième centenaire de la
naissance d'Honoré d'Urfé. Montbrison: La Diana,
1970. Aside from articles by M. Gehrhardt and M.
Debesse cited in notes, this volume includes excellent
studies by M. Laugaa on the role of painting in L'Astrée; by R. Lathullière on L'Astrée and the

"précieux" style; and by A. Pizzorusso on the Alcyre
episode.

Ehrmann, Jacques. Un Paradis désespéré: L'amour et
l'illusion dans "L'Astrée." New Haven: Yale University Press; Paris: PUF, 1963. Still the major critical work devoted to L'Astrée. While marked by the
quasi-existential vocabulary of its time, this study
remains a valuable contribution to understanding
L'Astrée.

Gaume, Maxime. Les Inspirations et les sources de
l'oeuvre d'Honoré d'Urfé. Saint-Etienne: Centre
d'Etudes foréziennes, 1977. A 760-page "summa" in
its own right offering everything—and more—on
d'Urfé's background, on the sources of all his works,
and on their general themes. Short on textual analysis per se, but nonetheless invaluable.

Genette, Gérard. "Le Serpent dans la Bergerie." In
L'Astrée, by Honoré d'Urfé. Paris: Union générale d'éditions, 1964. Collection 10/18. Reprinted
in Figures (Paris: Seuil, 1966), pp. 109-22. A
"classic" study of erotic intrusion into pastoral
bliss.

Germa, Bernard. "L'Astrée" d'Honoré d'Urfé, sa composition et son influence. Paris: Alphonse Picard,
1904. One of the major studies of L'Astrée, published at the time that modern scholars were "redis-
covering" d'Urfé. Dated, but still useful for principally historical questions.

Giorio, G. "L'Astrée" di Honoré d'Urfé tra barocco e
classicismo. Florence: La Nuova Italia, 1974.
Excellent bibliography. Short, thorough introduction
in Italian, focusing on narrative questions, on relationship of time and space, and on ties between the
baroque and classical novels.

Grieder, J. "Le Rôle de la religion dans la société
de l'Astrée." Dix-septième siècle, no. 93
(1972), pp. 3-12. Studies religion as counterpart to
cultural preoccupation of love, while establishing the
ultimately close relationship between druidism and
love theology.

Jehenson, Myriam Yvonne. The Golden World of the Pastoral. A Comparative Study of Sidney's "New Arcadia"
and d'Urfé's "L'Astrée." Ravenna, Italy: A.
Longo, 1981. The perspective of a comparatist, offering a short but rich analysis of L'Astrée. Helpful
for situating L'Astrée within a tradition. Views

Hylas's world as the intrusion of "reality" into Adamas's pure idealism.

Jourlait, Daniel. "La Mythologie dans L'Astrée." L'Esprit Créateur 16 (1976):125-37. Formulates interesting links between d'Urfé's use of mythology and the ideological, historical context of early seventeenth-century, aristocratic France.

Koch, Paule. "L'ascèse du repos ou l'intention idéologique de L'Astrée." Revue d'histoire littéraire de la France, nos. 3-4 (1977), pp. 386-98. Establishes the dialectic between calm and frenzy in L'Astrée, showing how the wobbly self-in-love is a negation of Stoic principles.

Laugaa, Maurice. "Structures ou personnages dans L'Astrée." Etudes françaises 2 (1966):3-27. Elaborately conceived and written analysis focusing on the function of poem and letter, on linearity versus simultaneity of the diverse narratives, and, generally, on L'Astrée as a "manipulator" of previously established literary forms.

McMahon, Sister Mary Catharine. Aesthetics and Art in the "Astrée" of Honoré d'Urfé. New York: AMS Press, 1969. A short but nonetheless satisfactory study in English of d'Urfé's intellectual background and of the composition of L'Astrée.

Magendie, Maurice. "L'Astrée" d'Honoré d'Urfé. Paris: Société française d'éditions littéraires et techniques, 1929. Published for "Les Grands Evénements Littéraires" series and clearly modeled on Magendie's earlier critical work on L'Astrée (see entry below), this book offers only introductory material on d'Urfé's life, on the story line of L'Astrée, and on the work's origins and influence. Helpful name index for characters.

_____. Du Nouveau sur "L'Astrée." Paris: Champion, 1927. Prior to Gaume's study, and along with Reure's book (see entry below), offers most thorough study of d'Urfé, of his minor works, and principally of the composition of L'Astrée. Focuses both on literary historical information and on textual analysis, the latter not always convincing. Banal in spots, lacking in bibliography, but still worth consulting.

Reure, O.-C. La vie et les oeuvres de Honoré d'Urfé. Paris: Plon, 1910. Part of the general "rediscovery" of d'Urfé occurring in the early decades of the twen-

tieth century.   Adheres faithfully to its title,
analyzing both background and composition.   Excellent
bibliographical material organized by chapter, and
helpful name and geographic indices.
Turk, Edward Baron.   Baroque Fiction-Making: A Study of
   Gomberville's "Polexandre."   Chapel Hill: North Caro-
   lina Studies in the Romance Languages and Literatures,
   1978.   Not devoted to L'Astrée in a formal fashion,
   but provides valuable insights on early seventeenth-
   century French fiction, particularly concerning structural matters.
Yon, Bernard, ed.   "L'Astrée"--VIème partie: La
   Suite de Gomberville.   Saint-Étienne: Presses de
   l'Université de Saint-Etienne, 1976.   Offers in addition to text a convincing and thorough introduction
   explaining the controversy over the sequels to
   d'Urfé's four volumes.

Index